THE FUTURE OF URBAN EMPLOYMENT

ILO
The future of urban employment
Geneva, International Labour Office, 1998

/Employment/, /Urban area/, /Employment policy/, /Developed country/, /Developing country/, /Rural migration/, /Informal sector/, /Unemployment/, /Poverty/, /Urbanization/, /Role of ILO/, /Employment creation/, /Local level/, /Social protection/, /Illustration/, /Reference. 13.01.3

ISBN 92-2-110337-4

Also available in French and Spanish

ILO Cataloguing in Publication Data

Designers: Enzo Fortarezza, Matteo Montesano and Valeria Morra
Printed in Italy by the International Training Centre of the ILO, Turin

THE FUTURE
OF URBAN
EMPLOYMENT

International Labour Office   Geneva

Governments should promote and pursue "active policies for **full, productive**, appropriately **remunerated** and **freely chosen employment**."

Programme of Action, World Summit for Social Development

PREFACE TO THE REVISED EDITION

The ILO's role in promoting employment and improving the quality of work was specifically acknowledged at the World Summit for Social Development held in Copenhagen in March 1995 **"because of its mandate, tripartite structure and expertise"**.

The original edition of this paper represented the ILO's contribution to the Second United Nations Conference on Human Settlements, and as such it has received broad recognition from the international press and from both national and municipal policy makers from around the world. Specifically, it served as a background paper to the Habitat II Dialogue for the 21st century on the Future of Urban Employment which the ILO organized in Istanbul in June 1996. This revised version of the paper, produced in response to continued high demand, provides updated data and overall policy guidance for the ILO's developing programme on urban employment.

The creation of equitable and productive employment is one of the most important global challenges that we face today. Over 1 billion people in the world at present live under unacceptable conditions of poverty. Creating and protecting employment is a key means of not only eradicating poverty but also of building a just, prosperous and stable society. The urbanization of the world, globalization and technological change, however, all present new dimensions to an old problem. Cities are increasingly at the forefront of these momentous changes, and despite their potential, are in many places of the world facing a crisis of unemployment, poverty, environmental degradation and the breakdown of urban services and infrastructure.

The coverage of this paper ranges from the focused to the general.* The focus is on **urban employment**: the underlying thesis is that creating and protecting employment can be the determining factor in easing if not resolving the multidimensional crisis faced by many cities worldwide. The subject is at the same time broad in that urban employment is a vast subject, encompassing both small and large cities, including mega-cities. Yet each city is different, and the reasons for the urban crisis are strikingly different from one city to the next and from one part of the world to another. This paper examines how global changes are being played out at the local level, the social ramifications of these economic transformations, and how employment will be the key to making cities humane places in which to live and work.

Samir Radwan
Director
Development Policies Department

*   The original edition of this paper, published in 1995, drew largely on an in-depth background document prepared by **Prof. Ajit Singh** of the Faculty of Economics of Cambridge University whose contribution is gratefully acknowledged.
The first edition was written by **Steven K. Miller** of the ILO and **Mr. Hoe Lim**, consultant. This edition was updated in 1997, with contributions from Jonathan Aspin, consultant.
The authors wish to thank the numerous colleagues who provided comments and contributions to this paper, and in particular:
Mr. G. Aryee,
Mr. B. Balkenhol,
Ms. C. Bengtsson,
Mr. J. Gaude,
Mr. M. Henriques,
Mr. A. Khan,
Mr. R. Kyloh,
Mr. E. Lee,
Mr. R. Lindenthal,
Mr. J.C. Liu,
Mr. C. Maldonado,
Mr. M. Mizuno,
Mr. G.B. Ng,
Mr. S. Oates,
Mr. A.S. Oberai,
Mr. J. Reichling,
Mr. S.V. Sethuraman,
Ms. C. Schylter,
Mr. H. Tabatabai and
Mr. R. Zachmann.

The opinions expressed here are those of the individual authors who collaborated in its preparation and do not necessarily reflect the views of the ILO.

EXECUTIVE SUMMARY

This paper presents the immense problems and the enormity of the tasks confronting those who lead the world's large cities, whether in the developing, transitional or industrialized worlds. There has been some convergence in the problems facing cities in all regions. Every first world city today has a third world city within it (immigrant ghettos and slums), and every third world city has a first world city (the modern skyscrapers, banks, the fashion-houses) within it. As globalization gathers pace, this convergence is likely to intensify as urban economies become increasingly integrated into the world economic system.

Trends in global urbanization and its implications for urban employment are discussed in the first part of this paper. By the end of the twentieth century nearly half of the world's population will be living in urban centres. Most of this shift will take place in the developing world, where rapid rates of urbanization have been experienced over the last 25 years. At present the world's urban labour force is growing at around 3% a year. In many parts of the world, not enough remunerative jobs are being generated to absorb new entrants into the labour market. In the industrialized countries, unemployment, which tends to be concentrated in urban centres, remains at very high levels. In the transitional countries, the shift towards a market-based system has resulted in severe job losses and economic hardship. These global trends have been paralleled by the urbanization of poverty.

The second part of this paper explores in greater depth the determinants of urban employment. Here, there is a paradox between cities as engines of economic growth and cities as centres of urban unemployment, poverty and other deprivations. This paradox is discussed in relationship to long-term economic growth and structural change, urban labour force growth and the operation of urban labour markets. First, while the industrialization of the developing world set in motion the process of urbanization there, this did not always achieve the levels of economic growth required to provide a rapidly growing urban labour force with remunerative employment. Second, unlike the experience of the industrialized countries and a few East Asian countries, urbanization and industrialization did not result in the disappearance of traditional or informal sector activities, nor in a major reduction in agricultural employment. Third, in the industrialized countries, urban centres have suffered disproportionately from the process of de-industrialization. At the same time, the growth in the service sector has not always provided new opportunities for displaced urban manufacturing workers, since these opportunities either require new skills or offer casual low-wage employment.

Fourth, the continuous flow of rural migrants to urban centres is often cited as one of the main causes of the problems faced by many cities in the developing world. It is frequently argued that urban problems cannot be resolved without first dealing with the development problems of rural areas. However, despite efforts to improve living standards in rural areas, migration to the cities continues unabated in many developing countries. Efforts to develop rural areas may have in some cases unintentionally encouraged migration. At the same time, natural population increase is now the dominant factor in the growth of the large cities. Equally, with globalization, international migration is also becoming a new and crucial element of the urban labour force.

Fifth, the failure of the modern private sector in the developing world to generate sufficient numbers of remunerative jobs has contributed to the growth of the urban informal sector. What was once thought to represent a transitory stage in the economic development process is now a major urban employer. In many cases, productivity and incomes are extremely low in the informal sector, and working conditions are very poor. This trend of continued informalization can also be seen in the industrialized countries where the downsizing of large enterprises, the introduction of flexible production technologies and service sector growth have led to increased numbers of part-time and casual workers.

Sixth, recent decades have seen the rapid introduction of new communication and production technologies and the liberalization of the world economic system. Cities will have to learn both to exploit the new opportunities created by the global market place and to respond to external shocks, the causes of which are likely to be beyond their control. At the same time, technological change is raising the much debated spectre of "jobless growth" and calls into question the assumed advantages of urban agglomeration economies. While the introduction of new technologies will create new jobs, cities cannot afford to be complacent and will need to create an environment which is conducive to inward investment.

The third part of this paper examines some of the key areas for policy intervention. In developing a framework for urban employment policy, attention is paid to the potential for new partnerships involving municipal authorities, national governments, workers, employers and civil society. It is noted that different strategies and tools are required for intervention at the international, national and local levels. For cities to be effective in creating and protecting employment through action at all three levels, they have to develop the necessary technical capacity for understanding the complexities of the international economy, and with the knowledge gained, to develop and implement local employment policies.

This part draws heavily on the ILO's work in this field, including policy advice and action programmes in the urban informal sector, employment-intensive investment policies, international labour standards, training and human resource development, cooperatives and enterprise development. Whereas the paper develops a certain number of policy prescriptions, they are by no means exhaustive and the examples given do not presume to present the whole picture. They are designed to stimulate thinking and facilitate further discussion. Recognizing that governments, especially at the municipal level, often feel helpless in the face of globalization, this section argues that policy-makers at all levels can take advantage of the opportunities available by building on local resources and expertise.

The final part of the paper draws together the various elements discussed and highlights the new challenges for urban employment policy in the twenty-first century. The three main issues raised are: the impact of technological change on job creation, employment structures and the location of industries and services; the role and capacity of local, national and international institutions in a global economy; and the growing informalization of work. Cutting across these issues is the fundamental question: to what extent and in which direction should the present policies and actions change, in specific countries and in the framework of international cooperation, in order to provide sustainable employment even in the poorest countries?

TABLE OF CONTENTS

List of figures

List of tables

List of boxes

1. THE URBAN CRISIS

1.1 Towards an urban world

1.   Urbanization is one of the major transformations of the twentieth century. By the end of the century, nearly half of humanity will be living in urban areas (see Figure 1). The most alarming aspect of this trend of global urbanization has been the pace at which it has occurred.

Most of the world's population will be urban dwellers

Figure 1:
Percentage of world population living in urban areas: 1950-2025

Source: UN (1997),
World Urbanization Prospects: The 1996 Revision, New York.

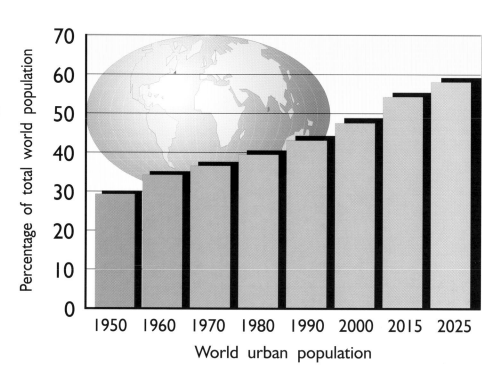

2.   The speed of urbanization has been particularly marked for the developing countries. In 1970, only a quarter of the population of developing countries lived in towns and cities. Twenty-five years later, this proportion had increased by a further half to reach 37.6%. It is estimated that by the year 2015, nearly 50% of the population of developing countries will be living in urban areas. In absolute terms, developing countries already account for the major share of the world's urban population (see Figure 2).

3.   There are however important regional differences in the degree of urbanization among developing countries (see Table 1). In Latin America and the Caribbean, the level of urbanization is now almost as high as that of industrialized countries. While the level of urbanization is much lower in Africa and Asia, the urban population in these two regions is growing at a much faster rate than elsewhere and will continue to do so for the foreseeable future.

4.   Contrary to popular perception, rural-urban migration is not the sole cause of the enormous expansion of all cities in the developing world. Between 1960 and 1970, for 26 large cities in the developing world, it is estimated that 63% of population growth was due to natural increase and 37% due to migration.[1]   However, causes of urban population growth cannot be easily generalized.   There are substantial demographic differences both within and between regions and countries. In Africa and parts of Asia, rural-urban migration is still a major factor in the urbanization process. It is also important to differentiate between large and small urban centres. In the latter case, much of the population growth is still accounted for by rural-urban migration. Ultimately, whichever is the dominant factor, solutions to urban unemployment cannot be adequately found without moderating urban population growth.

[1]   UN (1985), *Migration, Population Growth and Employment in Metropolitan Areas of Selected Developing Countries*, New York.

Developing countries account for the major share of the world's urban population
Figure 2: Share of the world's urban population

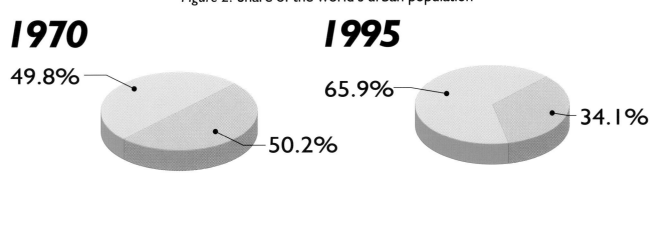

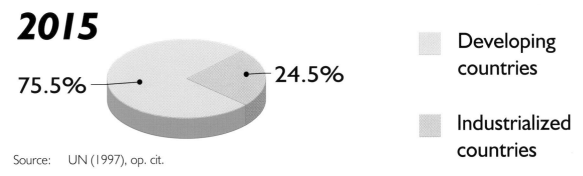

Source: UN (1997), op. cit.

Table 1:   **Urbanization in the developing world (% of total population)**

Major regions	1950	1970	1995
Africa	14.6	23.0	34.9
Asia	17.4	23.4	34.7
Latin America & Caribbean	41.4	57.4	73.4

Source: UN (1997), op. cit.

5.   While levels of urbanization are still the highest in the industrialized countries (80% or higher), there has since the 1970s been a consistent movement of population away from the large cities. This trend of counter-urbanization can be contrasted with developing countries, where "mega-cities" (population greater than 10 million) are rapidly forming. In 1950, there was only one city, London, with a population of more than 10 million. By 1995, of the 14 such cities in the world, 10 were in developing countries. Two decades from now, of the world's 26 largest cities with a population of 10 million or more, 22 will be in developing countries, and only four in industrialized countries.

"Mega-city" growth is a developing country phenomenon

Figure 3:
A world of cities
(Urban areas with populations above 10 million)

Developing countries

Industrialized countries

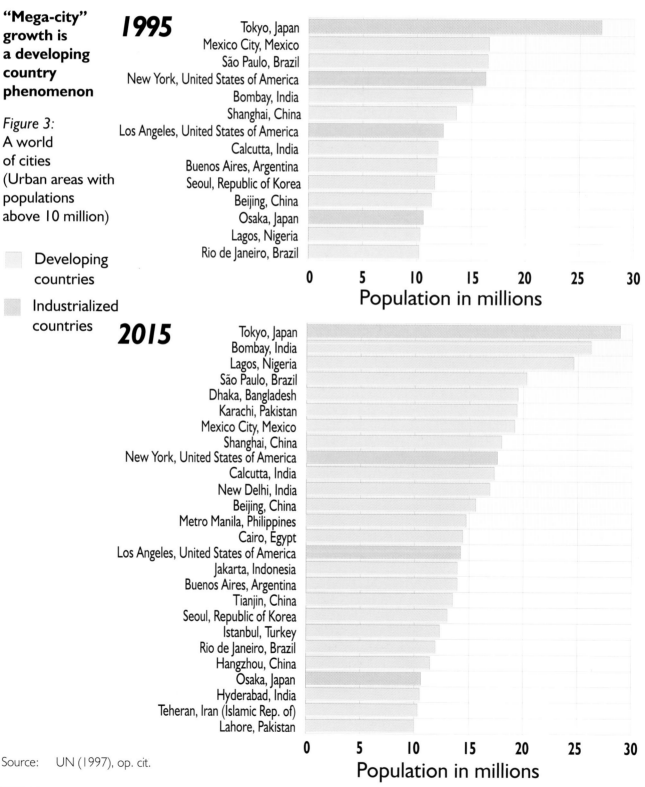

Source: UN (1997), op. cit.

1.2   Urban unemployment and poverty

6.   These demographic trends have important implications for urban employment and poverty in both developing and developed countries. A growing urban labour force is one of these implications. Estimates for the Asia-Pacific countries indicate that between 1980 and 1990, 40% of total labour force growth took place in urban areas. For 1990-2000, the corresponding proportion is expected to be 61%. By the period 2000-2010, urban labour force growth for the Asia-Pacific countries will represent 96% of all labour force growth. Translated into numbers of people, the urban labour force of these countries will grow by 328 million in the 20 years between 1990 and 2010.[2]

A growing urban labour force

[2]   UN (1993), *State of Urbanization in Asia and the Pacific*, New York.

Similar patterns and trends can be observed for other regions in the developing world. The problem of urban labour force absorption will be a major concern for many developing country cities, especially since many cities and countries throughout the world are experiencing a continuing economic crisis.

7.   The recorded rates of unemployment in most developing countries tend to be relatively low. This is because **unemployment in developing countries usually manifests itself in the form of under-employment**. In the virtual absence of a public social security system, people are obliged to engage in any economic activity, however non-remunerative and non-productive that may be. To illustrate, in 1988-89 in Ghana, the proportion of labour force unemployed was estimated at 1.6%. However, nearly a quarter of the workers were "underemployed", i.e., they worked less than full time, not because they chose to but because more work was unavailable (see Table 2).

Urban unemployment

Table 2:   **Unemployment and underemployment in selected countries**
        (Percentage of the labour force)

Country	Year	Unemployed	Underemployed[a]
Ghana	1988-89	1.6	24.1
Viet Nam	1992-93	1.3	10.0
Ukraine	1994	0.4	14.5

[a]   The definition of unemployed is conceptually and empirically problematic. In this table, the underemployed are defined as those working 15 hours or fewer per week.

Source: World Bank (1995), *World Development Report: Workers in an Integrating World*, Washington, D.C.

8.   In addition, the informal sector has become a major employer in many developing countries. In sub-Saharan Africa, the urban informal sector is estimated to employ over 60% of the urban labour force. In India and Pakistan, the unorganized segment of the manufacturing sector comprised approximately 75% and 70% respectively of total manufacturing in 1990. In Latin America, the share of employment in the urban informal sector increased from 13.4% of the labour force to 18.6% between 1980 and 1992.[3] The urban informal sector is considered in greater depth in the second part of this paper.

[3]   ILO (1995d), *World Employment Report 1995*, Geneva.

9.   Given the very high levels of urbanization in industrialized countries, unemployment is by and large an urban problem. In the European Union (EU), the unemployment rate was 11.4% in 1996, with double-digit unemployment rates in Belgium, Finland, France, Germany, Greece, Ireland, Italy and Spain, where nearly a quarter of the labour force is unemployed.[4] While the US has lower unemployment than the EU, average real wages have hardly increased over the last 20 years. Hence the problem is not just about creating jobs but about creating remunerative jobs.

10.   The dislocation of the whole system of central planning in the transitional countries has had severe implications for urban employment. Although precise data on urban areas are not available, national unemployment trends are most likely reflected at the urban level. By 1995, unemployment was between 10% and 15% in almost all the transitional countries of Eastern Europe.[5] Official unemployment rates do not however provide the full picture. Low or non-existent unemployment benefits have discouraged some unemployed people from registering. Instead, they have simply left the labour force, quite often to join the black economy . [6] Regional disparities have widened considerably. Youth unemployment has been rising sharply and it is likely that a vast number of teenagers and those in their early twenties could drift into a debilitating period of long-term unemployment or end up in the informal sector or the underground economy".

11.   Women workers tend to be particularly adversely affected by negative labour market trends. For instance, in Africa the rates of open unemployment for women are often double those for men and have been rising in recent years.[7] In the Asia-Pacific region, open unemployment rates for the mid-1980s to early 1990s have been higher for women than for men in China, Indonesia, Malaysia, Pakistan, Philippines, Thailand and Sri Lanka.[8] In the former East Germany, in 1991 women made up 62% of the registered unemployed, and many other women were known to have been pushed out of the labour force. In Russia, the female share of registered unemployment was even higher. In mid-1992, women made up a remarkable 78% of all the registered unemployed. In Poland, slightly less than half the registered unemployed were women. In the transitional countries of Eastern Europe, the effective labour force participation rate of women has been reduced by various indirect means, such as by the closure of enterprise-based or funded child-care facilities.[9]

12.   Given these trends, it is perhaps not surprising that at the International Colloquium of Mayors on Social Development held in New York, 1994, and again at the International Colloquium of Mayors on Governance for Sustainable Growth and Equity held in New York, 1997, urban unemployment was cited by mayors from all over the world as the number one problem facing their cities (see Figure 4).

[4]   IMF (1997), *World Economic Outlook*, October issue, p. 20, Washington, D.C.

[5]   ILO (1996), *World Employment Report 1996/97*, p. 111, Geneva.

[6]   ILO (1995d), op. cit.

[7]   In urban Kenya, 24.1% of women versus 11.7% of men were unemployed in 1991. In Egypt, the comparative rates were 27.8% for women and 6.3% for men. ILO (1995b), *Gender, Poverty and Employment*, p. 14, Geneva.

[8]   In Pakistan, for instance, during the period 1990-91 unemployment rates in urban areas were 27.8% for women versus 5.9% for men in urban areas. ILO (1995d), op. cit. p. 65.

[9]   ILO (1995d), op. cit.

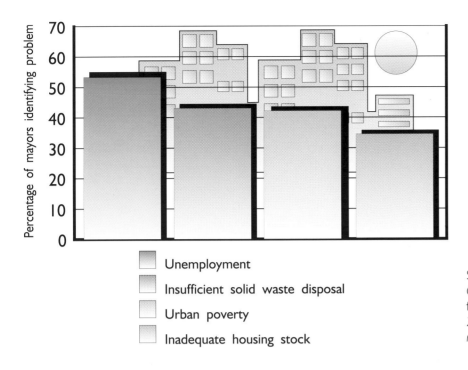

Unemployment and insufficient solid waste disposal identified as top urban concerns by mayors from both the developing and developed world

Figure 4:
Survey of 151 mayors from cities around the world, 1997

Source: UNDP (1997), *International Colloquium of Mayors on* Governance for Sustainable Growth and Equity, *28-30 July 1997, New York, press release.*

Note: 14 categories of "problems" were used in the survey of 151 mayors by UNDP. Mayors were permitted more than one choice.

Urbanization of poverty

13.   The lack of productive, appropriately remunerated and freely chosen employment is one of the most direct causes of poverty. In developing countries, the rise in urban unemployment and underemployment has been paralleled by the urbanization of poverty (see Table 3).

For instance, in Latin America, the annual rate of growth of urban poverty increased from 2.25% (1980-87) to 4.44% (1987-90). The rates of change for rural populations over the same periods were -0.42% and -2.16% respectively.[10] Nearly a third of the world's urban population is living in a state of absolute poverty. In 1990 this would have represented around 400 million people and the number is expected to grow to 1 billion by the end of the century. The incidence of urban poverty is highest in African cities and lowest in Asian cities.

[10]   De Janvry, et al. (1995), *Poverty and Rural Labour in South Asia, Latin America and sub-Saharan Africa*, ILO consultancy report (unpublished).

Table 3:   Incidence of urban poverty, 1988

Region	Urban population (million)	% share of total world urban population	Urban population below the poverty line	% of urban population below the poverty line	% share of the world's total number of urban poor
Africa	133.24	11.2	55.46	41.6	17.0
Asia	591.91	49.7	136.53	23.0	42.0
Latin America	174.14	14.7	59.53	34.2	18.0
Other regions	291.66	24.5	77.27	26.5	24.0
TOTAL	1191.95	100.0	329.79	27.7	100.0

Source: UN (1993), *State of Urbanization in Asia and the Pacific*, New York.

14.   Problems of urban poverty are not just restricted to developing countries. Overcrowding, hunger, disease, crime and malnutrition are increasingly a feature of inner city areas in some of the most advanced industrialized countries. This has led to a situation of tense segregation between rich and poor areas (see Box 1). In many transitional countries, the collapse of the centrally planned system has led to an appalling growth of poverty. In Bulgaria, for instance, statistics as of mid-1992 show that nearly 73% of all households had incomes below the official social minimum, up from 42% two years earlier. In the former USSR, by the end of 1991, about 100 million people were living below the poverty line, with average real family incomes in some areas being 26% below their levels at the beginning of the year.[11]

[11]   ILO (1995d), op. cit., p. 112.

Box 1:   **The "Citadel" cities of the developed world**

In its time Los Angeles has provided as much enthusiasm as any city on Earth. LA has grown more and more segregated and militarised. Starting at the outskirts, there is the Toxic Rim – a circle of giant garbage landfills, radioactive waste dumps and polluting industries. Moving inwards, you pass so called 'gated' or privately patrolled residential suburbs and a zone of self-policing lower middle-class homes, until you reach a 'free-fire' downtown area of ghettos and gangs. Here, the Ramparts Division of Los Angeles Police regularly investigates more murders than any other police department in the country. Finally, beyond this 'no-go area' lies the business district itself. In parts of this area, television cameras and security devices screen almost every passing pedestrian. At the touch of a button, access is blocked, bullet-proof screens are activated, bomb-proof shutters roll down. The appearance of the 'wrong sort of person' triggers a quiet panic. A new type of citadel has emerged.

Source: Rogers, R. (1995), "The BBC Reith Lectures", published in *The Independent*, from 13th February to 13th March, 1995.

15.   The urban poor usually have limited access to adequate shelter, education, health and social services. They are trapped in a vicious circle in which low incomes ensure poor education, nutrition and health, which in turn lead to low productivity and income. The urban poor also have greater health risks linked to the dangerous urban environment in which they live and work. The generation of productive employment is one of the keys to helping the poor to break this vicious circle. Box 2 provides an illustrative profile of the urban poor in Thailand, the characteristics of which apply to the urban poor in many other developing countries.

Box 2:   **The urban poor in Thailand**

Slum and squatter settlement surveys in Thailand in 1986 found that the urban poor have larger households (5.6 persons) and fewer income earners per household than the non-poor. They have older, less educated household heads and are less mobile than the non-poor. Those in larger cities were employed primarily as general labourers, production workers and street vendors. Those in smaller towns tended to be marginal farm operators. Though the urban poor derive a greater portion of their earnings from non-cash sources than the non-poor, this portion of income is still much less than that received through salary and wages. In order to make the most of their income, there is a strong reliance on self-produced food, clothing and household goods. Life patterns and livelihoods of the poor are spatially restricted to relatively small areas in the city, each of which has its own set of conditions and constraints. The poor, being less mobile than higher income groups, are more dependent on their immediate employment and living environment for their well-being. As a result, programmes to aid the poor need to respond to the specific local circumstances of the poor.

Source: UN (1993), op. cit.

2. DETERMINANTS OF URBAN EMPLOYMENT

2.1 Cities as engines of growth

16.   Despite all the enormous problems of poverty, unemployment and other deprivations of cities, they also embody for developing countries their hopes for the future. The serious problems of the urbanization process are only part of the picture. In general, the higher the level of a country's per capita income, the greater is its degree of urbanization and industrialization until a very high level of gross national product (GNP) per capita is reached (see Figure 5).

Figure 5:
Relationship between GNP per capita and urbanization

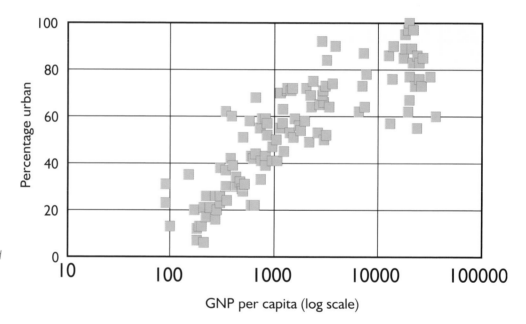

Source: Data from World Bank (1995), *World Development Report: Workers in an Integrating World,* Washington, D.C.

17.   However, this does not suggest a causal relationship between the two factors. Cities can grow without commensurate growth in per capita income and there are many cases where this relationship does not hold. For instance, between 1980 and 1993, sub-Saharan Africa had the highest rate of annual urban population growth in the world (4.8%) but negative rates of GNP per capita growth (- 0.8%). [12]

18.   Nevertheless, there are good reasons why cities should and do play a key role in economic growth. Some of these reasons are listed below:

- Infrastructure for modern industry – such as electricity, telecommunications, airports, etc. – comprises extremely expensive facilities. It is cheaper to centralize these services in a few strategic points.

- Easy availability of specialized business services that are essential for modern industry and business, and that can usually only be found in large cities.

[12]   World Bank (1995), *World Development Report: Workers in an Integrating World,* Washington, D.C.

- Availability of labour with a wide variety of skills – this is a feature of dense labour markets.

- The large-scale operations of firms lead to lower costs and better services which in turn improve the operations of other firms which purchase these goods and services. This process generates a virtuous circle of expanding markets and increased technical change.[13]

- A large city provides the focus of interaction for intellectual, business, cultural, political and religious elites.

[13] However, there are also costs in the form of congestion and pollution.

19.   It is due to these factors that **cities are regarded as engines of economic growth**. This is particularly true for cities in developing countries, since there are usually few alternative locations that can provide industry with the same benefits. It is thus not surprising to find that in large parts of the developing world, cities make a contribution to gross domestic product (GDP) that is disproportionate to their size. For example, although in terms of population Kenya is 23% urban, Nigeria 35% and India 27%, in all three countries the urban areas account for 70% of GDP.[14] Other examples are shown in Figure 6.

[14] World Bank (1991), *Urban Policy and Economic Development: An Agenda for the 1990s*, Washington, D.C.

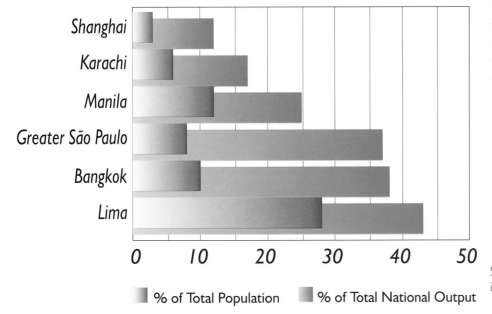

Figure 6:
Punching above their weight
(Comparing percentage of total population to national output)

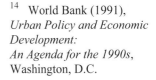
% of Total Population   % of Total National Output

Source: "A Survey of Cities", in *The Economist*, 29 July 1995.

However, if centralization is efficient and cities are engines of economic growth, why is it that they are increasingly unable in many parts of the world to deal with poverty, unemployment and underemployment? While there are no simple answers to this question, reflection on the relationship between long-term economic growth and structural change, and the operation of urban labour markets, can help shed some light on this apparent paradox.

2.2   *Structural change and urban employment*

20.   Long-term economic development is associated with a rise in the share of manufacturing in national output and a decline in that of agriculture. In turn the proportion of employment in agriculture declines while that in manufacturing steadily increases, until a very high level of per capita income is reached. In the very long term it is expected that labour will shift out of manufacturing into services. These are trends that generally hold true for most countries. But what does this mean for urban employment? In this respect, it is useful to consider the structural changes that have taken place in both developing and industrialized countries.

21.   Following the end of the Second World War, a modernization-oriented strategy was pursued by many developing countries. This was based on the assumption that the promotion of the urban industrial sector would be the key to accelerated growth. These policies were based on models of economic development which highlighted the incapacity of agriculture to indefinitely absorb labour and the importance of the modern manufacturing sector in generating output, income and employment. Consequently, a large number of developing countries embarked on their own industrial revolution. However, while some countries made considerable progress in establishing a technical, scientific and industrial infrastructure, in training their labour force and in developing a relatively broad-based industrial structure, others lagged seriously behind.

22.   On the whole, apart from the early success of Latin American countries and the "economic miracle" of a handful of East Asian countries, industrialization did not produce the expected results.[15] Nevertheless, the share of agriculture in total production in developing countries halved between 1960 and 1990 – from more than 30% to a little over 15%. There was a sizeable drop in every region, including Africa, where agriculture's share fell from a little over 45% to about 30% over this period. Here, there is a dilemma. Given that technical progress in agriculture is generally both labour saving and land saving, there is a limited capacity for this sector to absorb labour. In other words, even if agricultural output had increased, it is not certain that more jobs would have been generated. Industrialization should have been the means for solving this dilemma.

23.   While industrialization had set in motion the process of urbanization, it did not always achieve the levels of economic growth required to provide a rapidly growing urban labour force with productive employment.[16] Thus, unlike the experience of countries in Western Europe, the US and a few East Asian countries, urbanization and industrialization did not generally result in the disappearance of traditional or informal sector activities,[17] nor in a major reduction of employment in agriculture (see Table 4).

[15]   The reasons why many countries were not all that successful in industrializing are complex and beyond the scope of this paper.

[16]   Issues of rural-urban migration are examined in section 2.3.

[17]   In many developing countries, the informal sector continued to expand.

Table 4: **Structure of world employment, 1965 and 1989-1991 (%)**

	Agriculture		Industry		Services	
	1965	**1989-91**	**1965**	**1989-91**	**1965**	**1989-91**
World	57	48	19	17	24	35
Industrialized countries	22	7	37	26	41	67
Developing countries	72	61	11	14	17	25
East and South Asia [a]	73	50	9	18	18	32
Sub-Saharan Africa	79	67	8	9	13	24

[a] Figures for 1960 instead of 1965; industry comprises manufacturing only.

Source: ILO (1995d), *World Employment Report 1995*, Geneva.

24.   Structural change has also had important implications for urban employment in industrialized countries. Over recent decades, these countries have been undergoing a process of de-industrialization whereby the share of manufacturing employment and output have suffered a sizeable decline. In the UK, there were 7.9 million manufacturing workers in 1970; by 1993 this number had fallen to 4.3 million, a shrinkage of 46%. In France, the corresponding figure was 23%, in Germany 14% and the average for the Group of Seven large industrial countries was a fall of 15%. The service sector now accounts for the largest share of employment in industrialized countries as a whole (see Table 4). Cities have suffered disproportionately from the process of de-industrialization, since it is the urban areas that are the most heavily industrialized. While jobs have been created in the service sector, these have not always provided new opportunities for displaced urban manufacturing workers, since these opportunities either require new skills or offer casual low-wage employment. The difference with developing countries is that the industrialized countries have greater resources with which to deal with the problems of unemployment.

25.   The above analysis provides a framework for understanding how the fortunes of cities are linked with wider structural changes that affect national economies as a whole. These structural changes are in turn increasingly determined by international economic forces.[18] However, it is necessary to go further and to examine issues of employment at the level of the city. The following sections will briefly examine issues of urban labour force growth, urban labour markets and the role of the informal sector.

[18]   The dimension of globalization is examined in section 2.5.

2.3   *Rural-urban migration, natural population increase and the urban labour force*

[19] In general, the relative contributions of migration and natural increase vary according to existing levels of development and urbanization. In the initial period when urbanization levels are low and the rates of both urban and rural natural increase moderately high, the contribution of migration to urbanization tends to be more pronounced. In the intermediate stage, which practically characterizes the state in many of the more advanced developing countries today, natural increase predominates. At a latter stage, i.e., where there are mature urbanization and low levels of natural increase, net migration may again become relatively important. (See Oberai, A.S., 1993).

26.   Monitoring urban population growth is important as such growth is the direct determinant of future changes in the urban labour force. Urban population growth occurs in two ways: (a) through in-migration; and (b) through the natural rate of increase. The two are not autonomous but rather interrelated.[19]

27.   Although natural population increase is now cited as the major factor in large-city growth for many developing countries, there are major regional differences. In Africa and parts of Asia, the rural population is still significant. In these regions, there is still a great potential for further rural-urban migration. In the main, people migrate to urban areas for economic reasons (see Table 5 for main causes of migration). Thus, although beyond the direct control of municipal governments, the disparity between rural and urban areas, in terms of income and employment opportunities, is a factor that cannot be ignored by national planners concerned with economic development. Since the 1970s, rural development, often under the influence of the international development community, has been the focus of national development policy in many developing countries, and particularly in Africa. However, despite efforts to improve living standards in rural areas, migration to the cities continues unabated in many developing countries. Efforts to develop rural areas may have in some cases unintentionally encouraged migration. Improvements in education, infrastructure and basic services, all lead to the introduction of new skills, ambitions, values and standards, for which there is more scope and opportunity in an urban environment. This is not to say that these improvements should not be undertaken but that they do not offer immediate or easy solutions to a complex problem.

Table 5:   **Main causes of migration**

- Rural unemployment, underemployment and poverty
- Rapid population growth
- Inequalities in distribution of land and income
- Increasing landlessness
- Capital-intensive technology
- Urban bias in development policies
- Concentration of economic activities in urban areas
- Rural violence (conflicts, insecurity and social tensions)

Jacques Maillard, ILO Geneva

28.   The decentralization of industries to rural areas, with the objective of creating non-agricultural employment opportunities, has been tried in many countries. In China, for instance, programmes for establishing industries in rural areas and townships in the vicinity of urban centres have been particularly successful. In some cases, these effectively combined the development of modern high technology industries with small-scale labour-intensive production methods. The small-scale rural industrial (and service) firms have been able to produce both for the local market and for export.

29.   These programmes directed small savings into productive channels, stimulated entrepreneurship and contributed to the development of different skills.[20] By 1991, 1.44 million rural township and village enterprises had been established, employing around 47.7 million people. These industries have been successful not just in retaining the rural labour force but also in attracting urban labour.[21]

30.   However, programmes for creating rural industries will require a certain base level of supporting infrastructure. The costs of providing this can be prohibitively high in direct and indirect terms. First, urban unemployment is likely to rise as the most productive industries are decentralized to outlying areas. Second, there would be a loss in city revenue. These are both factors that have to be carefully evaluated in any policy for decentralization. Other policies that have been tried with varying degrees of success for controlling rural-urban migration include direct controls on population mobility, land settlement schemes, dispersed urbanization and rural development.

[20] Simai, M. (1995), *Global Employment: An International Investigation into the Future of Work*, Zed Books, Ltd., London and New Jersey.

[21] Liu, J. C. (1993). "Growth of employment in the informal sector in China: A review", ILO, Geneva, (unpublished document).

31.   The age composition of rural migrants has important implications for the growth and future composition of the urban labour force. Migration, as opposed to natural population growth, skews urban population growth towards the young as it is a selective process which tends to include those who are in the prime age group (i.e., between 15 and 35). These young migrants will be a direct addition to the urban labour force. They are also more likely to be starting families. They may regard having children as a form of social security against dire living and working conditions. This will fuel the natural urban population increase and in turn add to an increasingly young urban labour force in the foreseeable future. Ultimately, demand-side policies for employment creation need to be integrated with supply-side policies for controlling the natural population increase and rural-urban migration.

32.   Globalization is having important consequences on the pattern of urbanization and the internal structure of cities. International migration is a new and crucial element of the urban labour force, both in originating and receiving countries, highlighting the fact that urban unemployment is now a problem of global dimensions. International migration often leads to a "ratchet effect" on urbanization. Once international migrants return home from overseas employment, they are less likely to return to the rural areas from which they originated. The new tastes and experiences acquired overseas are likely to keep return migrants as new additions to the urban labour force at home.

33.   In recent years, though the rate of population increase has slowed from what it was in the 1970s, both the population and the labour force have increased in most urban centres. The formal absorptive capacity, on the other hand, has not displayed concomitant growth. Thus, where employment generation in the formal sector has lagged behind urban labour force growth, the excess supply has spilled over into the informal sector.

Jacques Maillard, ILO Geneva

2.4   *The urban labour market and the informal sector*

34.   Urban labour markets, especially in developing countries, have worked reasonably well, as judged by the migration of labour from rural to urban areas mainly in search of employment. However, inefficiencies and inequities still exist. Such outcomes in the urban labour markets are often attributed to "over-urbanization", meaning simply that increases in the supply of labour exceed increases in demand. The implication is that these markets are unable to adjust quickly. As a result three main trends have emerged in many developing countries:

- low-paid workers in the modern sector have been driven below the poverty line – this has forced them and members of their families to seek additional income through informal sector activities;

- workers are losing their employment in the modern sector – often as a result of government expenditure cuts in the public sector and/or stagnation of the private sector;

- increased numbers and intensified competition have driven people already in the informal sector down from the upper tiers – where they might have been on or above the poverty line – to below the poverty line.

35.   A substantial part of urban employment in many developing countries is in the public sector. By the early 1980s at least 15 African countries had 75 or more public enterprises. For a number of countries – Benin, Burkina Faso, Congo, Côte d'Ivoire, Ghana, Guinea, Malawi, Mozambique, Nigeria, United Republic of Tanzania, Togo, Zambia – public enterprises accounted for over 20% of formal sector wage employment.[22] In recent years, employment in the public sector has been under strain in many developing countries owing to pressure by structural adjustment programmes (SAPs) on governments to reduce public expenditure. Consequently public sector employment is stagnant if not on the decline.

36.   The "modern" private sector, which accounts for a substantial share of urban employment, is believed to be rising less rapidly, partly because of increasing capital intensity; employment increases are less than proportionate to increases in output. This is sometimes referred to as "jobless growth". The incapacity of the urban formal sector to create employment has shifted the burden of employment generation to the urban informal sector – a multitude of microenterprises mostly owned and operated by single individuals with little capital and skills. Adjustments in the urban labour market in many developing countries are therefore manifested in rising employment in the informal sector.[23] Indeed, informal sector activities are expected to provide 93% of all new jobs created in African cities in the 1990s.[24] In Latin America and the Caribbean, from 1990 to 1993, 83% of new jobs were created in the informal sector.[25] The exception has been the newly industrializing countries of East Asia where rapid output growth has resulted in growing formal sector employment. Here manufacturing employment grew by over 6% per year during the 1980s, and real earnings of workers rose by over 5% per year on average.

[22]   ILO (1995g), *World Labour Report 1995*, Geneva.

[23]   However, in sub-Saharan African countries, the growth of the urban informal sector has in recent years been paralleled by rising open unemployment.

[24]   ILO (1992b), *World Labour Report 1992*, Geneva.

[25]   ILO (1995f), *The Employment Challenge in Latin America and the Caribbean*, Working Paper No. 7, Lima.

37.   Urban labour markets may be segmented into not just two but several parts owing to institutional factors and rigidities. This is evident from the fact that the urban informal sector in developing countries is far from homogeneous. Incomes of workers in this sector vary considerably depending on the age, education, skills and sex of individuals, whether they are owners or employees in microenterprises, the type of activity and so on. It is also in part attributable to differential access to jobs and opportunities within the urban labour market. In addition, specific groups such as women face particular constraints that act as barriers to mobility from low to high productive activities.

38.   The net result has been not only low incomes of workers in the informal sector but also major variations between different groups. A strong overlap exists between urban poverty and employment in the informal sector. For example, in the late 1980s in Latin America, the proportion of urban poor (i.e., the bottom 20% ranked by per capita income) working in the informal sector was estimated to be as follows: Bolivia, 66%; Brazil, 66%; Costa Rica, 64%; Guatemala, 93%; Honduras, 85%; Panama, 87%; Paraguay, 65%; Uruguay, 18%; and Venezuela, 57%.[26] In sub-Saharan Africa, where two thirds or more of urban employment is in the informal sector, a vast majority is in the tertiary sector where incomes and productivity are extremely low.

39.   Urban employment in developing countries, especially in sub-Saharan Africa, has changed dramatically in recent years following the adoption of SAPs. Though they were aimed at achieving certain macro-economic objectives, such as price stability, they also affected the urban labour market by causing a decline in formal sector employment (most of which is located in and around the urban areas) and an increase in informal sector employment. Restrictive monetary and fiscal policies also frequently resulted in the decrease of wages and salaries (see Figure 7).

[26] Sethuraman, S.V. (1997), "Urban poverty and the informal sector", draft, ILO/UNDP.

Jacques Maillard, ILO Geneva

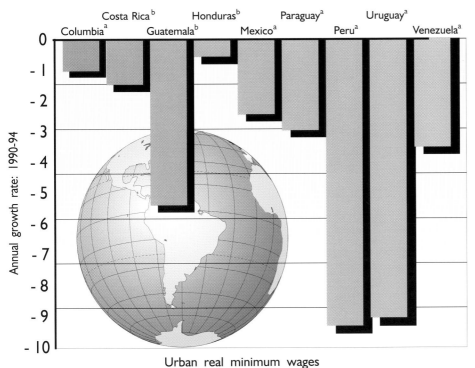

Figure 7:
Growth of urban real minimum wages – Latin America (selected countries)

[a] National minimum wages
[b] Lowest industrial minimum wages

Source: ILO (1995f), *The Employment Challenge in Latin America and the Caribbean*, Working Paper No. 7, Lima.

40.   Privatization also contributed to a decrease in public sector employment. Many of the retrenched workers had to turn to the informal sector. In fact, with declining real incomes, many formal sector employees had already been operating in the informal sector to supplement their incomes. In sub-Saharan Africa, where many countries have been implementing SAPs since the early 1980s, urban informal sector employment is estimated to have risen at 6.7% per year between 1980 and 1985. In Latin America too, the share of the informal sector in total urban employment rose during the 1980s.[27, 28]

41.   In the context of globalization, liberalization of trade – including foreign exchange deregulation – may have encouraged the expansion of tertiary activities, especially petty trading. Some microentrepreneurs, particularly those with more education, skills and prior experience in the formal sector, may have benefited from the SAPs because they were able to adapt and successfully exploit the new opportunities. On the whole, in recent years, **the urban employment structure has changed in the direction of more employment in low-income activities, and increasing urban poverty**.

[27] In Venezuela, from 23% in 1979 to 32% in 1987; in Mexico, from 24% in 1980 to 33% in 1987; and in Bolivia, from 52% in 1985 to 58% in 1989.

[28] Sethuraman (1997), op. cit.

Jacques Maillard. ILO Geneva

42.   Many in the informal sector not only hold precarious employment but are also highly vulnerable to exploitation. They are often obliged to seek alternative mechanisms of integration with the mainstream economy because they are denied access to resources and markets through the normal channels and because they lack skills and capital. In certain countries women resort to sub-contracting work from other firms or middlemen at low levels of remuneration, and often lack adequate social protection.

43.   Issues concerning the urban labour market and the informal sector are usually analysed within the context of national economies. However, with globalization there is increasingly an international economic dimension which has also to be considered. International debt problems, the introduction of SAPs, the pace and pattern of industrialization and de-industrialization, are all factors that are fundamentally linked to international economic forces. Neither national nor urban economies can choose to ignore these linkages. At the same time, technological change and the liberalization of trade and investment have made possible a whole range of complex, yet flexible, patterns of sub-contracting. These international production processes affect not just the urban formal sector, but also the urban informal sector. Some of the main implications arising from these changes are examined in the following section.

2.5 Globalization and technological change: Implications for the future of urban employment

44. An outstanding feature of the world economy during the recent period has been globalization, a term which normally connotes three things: (a) freer trade between countries in goods and services; (b) freer movements of financial capital; and (c) removal of restrictions on foreign direct investment (FDI). The globalization process started in advanced countries with the deregulation of financial markets in the late 1970s. It gathered pace in the 1980s with the virtual abolition of exchange controls among most industrial countries. In the 1990s, liberalization of financial markets has become a worldwide phenomenon, and it now involves a large number of developing countries as well. For a variety of reasons, this external liberalization has gone hand in hand with internal liberalization, particularly of labour markets in many countries. The whole process was given further impetus by the Uruguay Round Agreements of 1994, which provide for freer trade, not just in manufactures but also in agriculture and services.

45. Globalization has important implications for the future of cities and urban employment. These include both opportunities and risks. First, as economies become more interdependent, it is not only the opportunity for wealth creation that is multiplied, but also the opportunity for destabilizing shocks to be transmitted from one country to another. These shocks can have devastating effects on cities, since the bulk of economic activity is located there. Second, the creation of a global market-place will mean more competition not just between countries but also between cities. The ability to attract business investment is an important factor in determining the success of urban economies. As national barriers to the movement of capital come down, cities will increasingly be pitted against each other as they compete for inward investment. Success or failure will depend very much upon the ability of municipal governments to provide the type of infrastructure services and human capital that are required by modern businesses.

46. Whether globalization is a positive trend or not, one thing is clear: both national and urban economies will display greater instability, and be subjected to greater external economic shocks and competition than before. Cities will have to learn to live with these conditions. If the proponents of globalization are right, there would be compensation in the form of faster economic growth and more jobs. But at this point, it is very much an open question as to whether these favourable outcomes will actually materialize. However, the picture is not completely bleak. The challenge for municipal governments is to make the most of the employment opportunities presented by globalization, through ensuring that their resources are not left to stagnate or decline in the face of a highly competitive international economic environment.

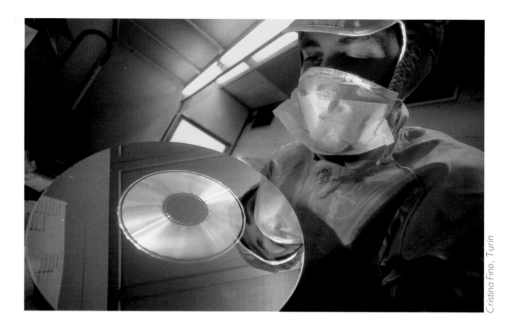

Cristina Fino, Turin

47.   Linked to globalization is the fact that the twentieth century has been a century of astounding technological change. The rapid advances made, especially in the field of information and communications technology, have resulted in:

- a wide range of new products;
- a fall in costs and vastly improved technical performance in many sectors of the economy;
- fundamental changes in the organization, management and production structure of firms and industries;
- a reduced need for spatial proximity.

There are a number of important implications on urban employment that arise from the introduction of new technology:

- What will be new sources of economic growth and where will they be located?
- What will this imply for the economic role of cities?

48.   Answers to these questions hinge upon whether the pace of technological progress has become so fast that we are observing jobless growth – i.e., economic growth that does not create any employment at all, or in a less extreme form, a situation where a given percentage change in economic growth leads to a smaller increase in employment than used to be the case. The fear that machines will replace workers has waxed and waned since the beginning of the industrial revolution in Europe. At present, fear is growing strongly with prophecies that the "end of work" is nigh. There is concern that recent technical change has been skill-biased and has greatly reduced the demand for low-skilled workers. This bias is seen as a major cause both of the rise in unemployment and its concentration among low-skilled workers, and of the rise in wage inequalities between the skilled and the low skilled.[29] However, technical progress has dual effects. On the one hand, it may replace labour with capital. On the other, it lowers costs and creates new products and services

[29]   Lee, E. (1995), "Overview of the special issue: Employment policy in the global economy", *International Labour Review*, Vol. 134, No. 4-5.

– which in turn generates employment. Depending on the balance between these two effects, technical progress can be either job-destroying or job-creating for the economy as a whole. It is thus uncertain whether the introduction of new technology will make labour redundant, or whether it will provide an impetus for reinvigorating economic growth and hence employment.

49.   The impact that information and communications technology has had on the advantages arising from spatial proximity represents another important implication for urban employment. Will this technology erode these advantages and thereby reduce the competitive advantage of large cities? There is no firm evidence on this subject and the general view seems to be that it is unlikely to have a serious impact on the advantages offered by large cities, particularly in developing countries. However, in many industrialized countries there has been a consistent trend of large firms decentralizing their administrative support functions away from capital cities to smaller towns, leaving behind only a small core of high-level staff. Industries are also becoming more "footloose" and are less bound to specific geographical areas. Indeed, in many industrialized countries the problems of urban unemployment have much to do with a combination of old industries closing down and new industries setting up elsewhere. Improvements in information and communications technology have all played an important part in allowing these shifts to occur. This has led to an increased flow of FDI, as well as to a rise in global "electronic outworking" in the form of the transfer of data entry, processing and computer programming to developing countries.

50.   While an agglomeration of high-tech firms, such as "Silicon Valley" in California, may be an exceptional case, cities cannot ignore the implications that further technological progress in information and communications will have on the nature of work and the distribution of economic activities. Indeed, in the case of major cities such as New York, Tokyo and London an emerging thesis is that they will gain even greater prominence as global cities with a high concentration of financial and producer services.[30] Nevertheless, the sheer variety of skills, services and infrastructures still gives cities a certain advantage. However, local governments cannot afford to be complacent. Congestion, pollution, poor infrastructure and inefficient public services are all factors that can rapidly undermine any advantages that are gained from spatial proximity.

[30] Sassen, S. (1991), *The Global City*, Princeton University Press, Princeton.

51.   However, the lesson to be drawn is that cities are now linked together in an interdependent web of trade and communications, and the future of one city may now be intricately tied to the future of another. Production processes are no longer as bound to geographical constraints as before. Goods can be assembled in one part of the world, then transported to another for packaging and then shipped back again for sale. Similarly, rapid advances in telecommunications are making it possible to decentralize service functions to where the costs are lowest. When major international airlines are decentralizing their reservations and budgetary sections to other parts of the globe, it becomes clear that the world is becoming more and more a global village. The next part will address what can be done at the local level to create employment in such a rapidly changing and urbanizing world.

3. A FRAMEWORK FOR URBAN EMPLOYMENT POLICY

3.1 Levels of intervention

52.   It is an inescapable fact that globalization, macro-economic trends and the world economy have an overriding impact on employment creation in our cities. Policy decisions that were formerly made at the national level are currently being circumscribed by events at the international level. Yet this does not mean that national governments, municipal policy-makers, workers, employers and civil society are helpless in the face of world events. **Although they certainly have to understand and accept certain economic facts of life this knowledge can provide the springboard for jumping into the global economy**.

53.   What can workers, employers and governments do to create new employment opportunities, and better protect existing employment, in a globalizing world? If urban employment is the key to solving other problems faced by municipalities, how can a strategy to create employment build on the comparative strengths of actors at the municipal and local levels?

54.   The potential for new partnerships raises the issue of levels of policy intervention in which municipal authorities can play a role. Briefly, they can:

- at the international level, understand and influence global economic policies;
- at the national level, affect macro-economic and other national policies towards cities; and
- at the city level, affect employment prospects through a range of local economic and social development measures.

55.   Each of these levels requires different strategies and tools for implementation. Responding to globalization needs a global partnership among mayors. Associations of municipalities, such as the International Union of Local Authorities, are gaining strength and recognition on the world scene. They can play a role in influencing policies, not only of their respective national governments, but also at international economic and social policy fora. By joining hands with organizations of workers and employers, including private sector employers, their influence would be further strengthened. The International Colloquiums of Mayors, held in New York in 1994 and 1997, and the many meetings associated with the Habitat II Preparatory Process are examples of where associations of local authorities have already spoken out.

56.   Of course, for cities to be effective in creating and protecting employment through action at all three levels, they have to develop the necessary technical capacity for understanding the complexities of the international economy, and for developing and implementing local employment policies. As it now stands they are often preoccupied with damage limitation, simply trying to cope passively with all the negative consequences of urban unemployment such as poverty, violence, drugs, homelessness, street children, and lack of city resources. Developing the institutional capacity of local level actors will be the action-oriented focus of the following sections. Specifically, they will concentrate on areas of strength, where local authorities, in partnership with other key actors, can make a difference.

3.2   Strengths of local authorities for creating employment

57.   The first strength results from the growing tendency towards **decentralization of responsibilities and resources** to the municipal level. New legislation is being enacted in a wide range of countries from all regions giving municipal governments these new powers and resources. The main problem that municipalities often face is that they are given the responsibilities without the corresponding resources. Nevertheless, municipalities can take advantage of this trend towards decentralization to play a more active role in creating new jobs. If city governments are to be involved in employment-generation activities, they must be given a clear mandate from central government together with the necessary financial support. However, while it will be efficient for cities to take over many of the economic functions at present performed by central governments, their technical capacity would need to be enhanced. Measures are thus required to strengthen local governments, often in areas such as investment policy and economic planning where in the past they did not have the authority to act.

58.   The questions of governance and civic engagement are at the heart of the process of decentralization. Governance is the sum of the many ways in which individuals and institutions, public and private, manage their common affairs. It is a continuing process through which conflicting or diverse interests may be accommodated and cooperative action may be taken. There is no single model or form of governance, nor is there a single structure or set of structures. There are, however, a number of principles that relate to the concept of governance, namely, transparency, accountability, consultation, collective participation and democracy. The challenge for municipal governments is to ensure that these principles are embodied in their work on employment creation and poverty alleviation.

59.   The second area of strength concerns the **regulatory framework**. Land regulations, public and private contracting procedures, zoning laws, registration of enterprises, including micro-enterprises and street vendors, can all be influenced, if not fully determined, at the local level. Local authorities can also support and implement labour standards, a crucial element in improving both the quantity and quality of employment. Whereas international deregulation has opened up cities to both the pitfalls and windfalls of a global market, the regulatory environment can be managed creatively at the local level, not just to protect local employment, but also to take advantage of opportunities which did not exist previously in a world of protected national economies.

60.   A third area of strength is the ability of municipalities to **forge new alliances and create partnerships** for employment creation. "Enablement" has been one of the guiding principles of human settlements policies in recent years and of the Habitat II Conference. Enablement carries a recognition of the fact that municipalities can no longer be expected to provide municipal services, infrastructure, housing and employment to urban populations single-handedly. Rather, municipalities can benefit from the strengths – and resources – of other actors present at the local level. Such key actors include workers' and employers' organizations, the private sector, non-governmental organizations, community advocacy groups, informal sector associations, community contractors, and other community-based organizations. By working in partnership with these groups, as well of course as with national governments, and even with international organizations, municipal governments are now better able to face up to the challenge of urban employment than they would be if acting in isolation.

61.   Just as it is desirable to decentralize decision-making from the centre to the cities, it is similarly useful to decentralize power within the city itself. The city is a complex organism and it is important for people to be as directly involved in the running of its affairs at all levels as far as it is practical. This is particularly important for those who live in slums and poor areas, as they have less political power and ability to articulate their concerns than middle or upper income groups. Involvement of business groups, trade unions, various informal sector associations and neighbour-hood committees in the day-to-day decision-making of the city should lead to more informed decisions, more democratic governance and a greater role for civil society. It should also enhance accountability and check bureaucratic tendencies within local government. Since a large proportion of poor households in urban areas are headed by women, it is especially important that women's groups be well represented and participate fully in such community organizations and in interactions with local government.

3.3 An agenda for local action in a world economy

62.   In focusing on the comparative strengths of the local or municipal levels, it should not be forgotten that **national governments still have heavy responsibilities** and – in many developing countries – still the majority of the resources required to create employment. Decentralization will require a common understanding and mutual trust between national and local governments. Privatization of municipal services such as street repair or garbage collection, for example, does not imply a weakened public sector, but rather a changed role in which the public sector may have to be strengthened in its ability to contract out and supervise implementation, rather than to provide the services itself. Similarly, decentralization may require enhancing the capacity of national governments to live up to and act within the confines of this new relationship.

63.   In other cases, particularly in national capital cities, responsibilities between national and local governments may be blurred. Municipal governments simply may not have the resources to provide even the most basic municipal services, not to mention infrastructure investments. Municipal governments may be overly dependent on the national government, thereby weakening both the national government (by draining resources and expertise away from its national-level responsibilities and fuelling criticisms of "urban bias") and the municipalities (by weakening their ability to mobilize resources and create partnerships at the local level).

64.   Ultimately, national governments have an important role in establishing the overall economic environment within which the urban economy operates. While municipal governments can improve policy-making at the city level, their policies can have only a limited impact on levels of income and productivity unless they are accompanied by appropriate macro-economic policies designed to regenerate overall economic growth.

Role and capacity of national governments

Jacques Maillard, ILO Geneva

Areas of local government action

65.   *The following framework builds on the comparative advantages of local governments* in the field of employment promotion and social protection. It will point to areas of local government action in the following areas:

- investment policies for employment-intensive shelter development;
- policies to increase productivity, incomes and social protection for the urban informal sector;
- the regulatory environment as a facilitator for job creation and improved working conditions; and finally
- new alliances to mobilize resources for direct action.

66.   These four areas are by no means exhaustive, nor mutually exclusive. In fact most of them overlap. Within this framework it is important to differentiate between policies best developed at the city level and those at the national level. Table 6 provides an indicative list of policy actions at city and national levels for employment promotion.

Table 6:   **Policy actions at city and national levels for employment promotion**

Actions at the city level	Actions at the national level
● Reorientation of public expenditure	● Devolution of authority to city administrations
● Improvements in public service delivery	● Improved sharing of resources
● Removal of constraints in public administration, regulation and taxation that inhibit the operation of small enterprises	● Reduction of fiscal and other policy biases that favour large, modern sector enterprises
● Location of schools and health centres in areas of high social exclusion	● Forging greater linkages between large and small enterprises
● Promotion of efficient and fuller utilization of industrial and social service infrastructure	● Removal of urban or anti-urban bias in economic and social policies (e.g., price distortions, trade protection, location of industries)
● Improvements in land tenure	
● Rent control reforms	
● Control of land speculation and promotion of rational use of vacant urban land	
● Promotion of community organization and participation in self-help schemes	
● Cost recovery through user charges	

In the following sections, the possibilities for maximizing the areas of local comparative advantage in the implementation of these and other policies are discussed.

3.4 Employment-intensive investment policies

67. Investment policies are perhaps the most powerful tool at the disposal of municipal authorities for job creation. Investments in basic infrastructure can provide cities with the competitive edge required to attract new industries in the global market-place. Basic amenities govern whether or not cities are desirable places to live. Infrastructure provides employment opportunities during its construction, and in its operation and maintenance. Infrastructure is not just factories, power plants and airports, but also basic services required by all urban dwellers to live and work in the city.

68. On the whole, developing countries invest US$200 billion a year in new infrastructure – 4% of their national output and a fifth of total investment.[31] Infrastructure is one of the keys to economic growth and correspondingly to the expansion of productive employment. Even in times of stagnant or sluggish economic growth, decisions made concerning the allocation of scarce resources to infrastructure can have a major impact on employment creation. Infrastructure investment policies used to be in the domain of national-level policy-makers. However, with policies for decentralization, infrastructure investments are being controlled more and more at the level of municipalities. In Argentina, provinces and municipalities are responsible for elementary and secondary education, health care, water and sewerage, regional and local roads, solid waste collection and disposal, local streets and drainage.[32] International financial institutions such as the World Bank are increasingly providing finance directly to municipalities for infrastructure development. In developed countries, municipal resource mobilization through bonds and other investment funds is common.

69. However, infrastructure investments are often misallocated, and provide services at the wrong standard.[33] Also, many costly infrastructure investments such as power or water supply systems are operating well below their best practice capacity due to inadequate maintenance, whereas other services, particularly those touching poor urban settlements, are either non-existent or inadequate as related to the urban poor's willingness and ability to pay. Thus while, on aggregate, urban areas appear to be better served than rural areas, in reality due to unequal distribution there is a great divide between those who have access to these services and those who do not. In fact, for many basic services such as water supply and sanitation, those urban poor who do not have access to these services may actually be paying a higher price than the more well-to-do population that do have access (see Box 3). In addition, in many cases segments of the urban population who are served by public services are paying less than the recovery cost. There is thus a need to extend public services to marginalized urban communities while ensuring that cost-based user charges are collected from those served. Therefore, there is considerable scope for increasing the impact of infrastructure investment resources on job creation and poverty alleviation. This employment effect can be ensured by choosing more labour-intensive alternatives and by giving priority to secondary and tertiary infrastructure which is more labour-intensive by nature. Participation of local populations, furthermore, enhances the viability and impact of investments.

Creating and protecting employment through infrastructure and shelter

[31] World Bank (1994), *World Development Report: Infrastructure for Development*, Washington, D.C.

[32] See Vetter, D. (1995), "Financing of human settlements by subnational governments: Opportunities for international cooperation", paper presented at the Conference on Human Settlements in the Changing Global Political and Economic Process, Helsinki, Finland, August 27, 1995.

[33] World Bank (1994), op. cit.

Box 3:   **The poor pay more**

Relative to what they earn, the poor usually pay higher prices for food, water, shelter, clothing and credit than those who are better off. For instance:

- In Nouakchott, Mauritania, the poor frequently have to buy water from a water merchant, with no guarantee as to quality and with the price up to 100 times that paid by those with piped water connections.
- In Guayaquil, Ecuador, drinking water supplied by tank to slum areas costs 20 times more than that to piped areas.
- In Cali, Colombia the urban poor buy water of sub-standard quality from inefficient private vendors at prices 10 times higher than could be provided by local authorities.
- Studies of housing consumption patterns in developing countries have found that the poor inevitably pay a higher proportion of their incomes for housing than do better-off households.

Sources: World Bank (1991), *Urban Policy and Economic Development: An Agenda for the 1990s*, Washington, D.C.; Caplowitz, D. (1967), *The Poor Pay More*, Free Press, New York; Harpham, T., et al (1988), *In the Shadow of the City: Community Health and the Urban Poor*, Oxford University Press; Mazo, S., et al, (1986), "Shelter strategies for the urban poor in developing countries", in *World Bank Research Observer*.

[34] A study of gravel road construction in Burkina Faso showed that labour-intensive techniques, when compared with highly mechanized alternatives, cost 42% less in financial terms for a road of comparable technical standard, while at the same time creating 75% more employment, not to mention savings in foreign currency. See Imschoot, Marc van (1993), "Burkina Faso: Note sur les modalités de mise en place de la composante HIMO du PASECT du projet d'assistance PNUD/BIT – BKF/87/011, avril 1993".

70.   Changes are required at a number of different levels. Municipal technical services must understand that labour-intensive methods can be a cost-effective and high-quality alternative to equipment-based methods, particularly in situations where wage rates for unskilled labour are relatively low.[34] Training for municipal technical services is often necessary since equipment-based methods are those commonly known and taught within technical schools. Likewise, procedures need to be adapted to encourage labour-based small contractors to bid on municipal contracts for infrastructure development. Pre-qualification requirements such as equipment possessed, size of contracts and complicated tendering and bidding procedures can effectively discriminate against adoption of labour-based contracting.

71.   Finally, those infrastructure investments which are of greatest benefit to the urban poor, such as drainage, erosion control, waste management and sanitation, are all conducive to labour-intensive technologies and provide direct improvements to the **urban environment**. Likewise, investments in non-motorized urban transport are beneficial, not only to accessibility and productivity of informal sector enterprises working out of informal settlements, but also help reduce air pollution and traffic congestion, thereby improving the urban environment.

> ### Box 4:   Increasing the employment impact of national investment policy
>
> An ILO study covering the three West African countries of Côte d'Ivoire, Senegal and Burkina Faso states that 31%, 43% and 63% respectively of the total public investment budget went into the building and public works sector. It was estimated that labour accounted for approximately 15% of the total factor costs of these investments. However, the study also pointed out that there was considerable untapped potential for undertaking many types of infrastructure with more employment-intensive technologies without compromising either cost-effectiveness or technical standards. In the case of Senegal, a realistic objective of increasing the labour component of public works investments from 10% to 25% would result in the creation of approximately 10,000 jobs.
>
> Source: ILO (1994a), Geneva.

Employment impact of shelter

72.   Shelter refers to more than just housing. Shelter involves a whole range of infrastructure associated with human settlements and with healthy, safe and productive living and working conditions. Investing in shelter creates jobs, improves productivity and raises incomes. Increased shelter development activities trigger additional investments in building materials production, transport and marketing. These in turn generate demand in other sectors. Any investment in housing or infrastructure can thus have a multiplier effect that extends beyond the housing sector (see Box 5). Evidence from a number of countries indicates that for every unit of currency spent directly on housing construction, an additional unit of currency is added to the national income.

73.   Low-cost or informal sector housing, as well as being more labour-intensive than formal sector housing, may also be a more effective means of providing shelter to poor urban communities. Formal sector housing usually cannot be afforded by the poor. In many cases, low-cost housing, although officially intended for the poor, is usually taken up by middle and high income households. In Thailand, for instance, alternative low-cost housing projects run by the National Housing Authority were too expensive for the poorest urban residents. As a result, about 70% of the eligible low-cost housing dwellers sold their rights to higher-income families while they returned to squatter-slum areas.[35] In Zambia, which has one of the highest rates of urbanization in Africa, informal sector housing produces six times as many dwellings (though of lower standard) for the same investment as formal sector housing and is more easily afforded by the urban poor.[36]

[35]   UN (1993), op. cit.

[36]   Tournée, J. and Omwanza, J. (1995), "Alternative strategies for the provision of infrastructure in urban unplanned settlements", in ILO, *Labour-based Technology – A Review of Current Practice*, Vol. 2.

Box 5: **Housing construction – income and employment generation effects**

Housing investment gives rise to investment in other sectors because the construction sector is a significant purchaser of goods and services from other sectors. For most countries, investments in the housing sector account for between 2% and 8% of GNP and between 10% and 30% of gross capital formation. Research shows that backward linkages in the construction sector are greater than in most other sectors.* In Mexico, for example, the ratio of direct to indirect employment in the construction sector was 10:7. The choice of materials plays an important role in the employment creation potential of the construction sector: the simpler the materials, the more local and small-scale enterprises will be involved in supplying them.

The employment opportunities of the building industry depend on the development level of the country. In the case of Kenya, housing construction creates large amounts of direct employment (currently some 12,000 work years), because its labour content is relatively high. On average, each K.$ 1 million spent on housing in Kenya means one year's full-time employment for 2,000 people.

* Backward linkages are measures of those demands created by one economic sector (in this case construction) for the products of other sectors. In construction, they are mainly involved in the building operation, and before that, the production of materials, transport and other activities prior to building.

Sources: Ministry of Foreign Affairs, The Netherlands (1994), *Urban Poverty Alleviation*, The Hague; UNCHS/ILO (1995), *Shelter Provision and Employment Generation*, Nairobi and Geneva.

The home as a workplace

[37] ILO (1995d), op. cit.

[38] Tipple, G. (1993), "Shelter as workplace: A review of home-based enterprise in developing countries", in *International Labour Review*, Vol. 132, No. 4.

74.   The employment effects of housing go well beyond the construction and maintenance of housing. The home is also a workplace, particularly for women, in developing countries. The work undertaken can range from the retailing of food to garment making and other light industrial activities.[37] If there is one lesson for planners in the massive literature on slums and squatter community life, it is that housing in these areas is not for home life alone. A house is a production place, a market-place, an entertainment centre, a financial institution and also a retreat. Both the home and the community derive their vitality from this multiplicity of uses. The imposition of artificial restrictions on both would only hinder their development.[38]

75.   Improving and increasing the housing supply in informal settlements can thus be a direct means of supporting small- and micro-scale enterprises. However, while home-based enterprises can make an important contribution to the livelihoods of the poorest households, it is necessary to ensure that both functions of work and home are accommodated in a safe and environmentally acceptable manner. Indeed, better housing may directly improve working conditions. Apart from improving physical conditions, measures are also required to help homeworkers to organize against exploitation by sub-contracting firms (see Box 6).

Jacques Maillard, ILO Geneva

Box 6: **Women homeworkers – the invisible workforce**

The pursuit of flexible low-cost labour has encouraged industrial enterprises to resort to sub-contracting with concomitant extension of home work and other forms of outwork. In the vast majority of cases, homeworkers are women – often with small children. These women are usually forced into such activities because of their family responsibilities and the lack of other income-earning opportunities. Being largely invisible and difficult to organize, homeworkers are particularly vulnerable to exploitation and are often excluded from the protection and benefits afforded by labour legislation.

For instance in Fortaleza, one of the largest cities in the northeast of Brazil, there is a growing workforce in the hammock industry that is based at home. Registered factories use unregistered homeworkers as it is a considerable saving for them. One factory visited in 1978 had seven registered employees but several hundred people on sub-contracts working at home. This may be an extreme case but virtually all hammock-makers put out work to people working at home – usually women. However, working on hammock finishing at home, even where this is done full time, produces substantially less than the minimum wage. A survey of homeworkers (conducted in 1993) in Viet Nam shows that they usually work very long hours (an average of 55 hours a week) and in a good month homeworkers can expect to earn around only US$59.

Sources: ILO (1995b), *Gender, Poverty and Employment: Turning Capabilities into Entitlements*; Hardoy, J. and Satterthwaite, D. (1995), *Squatter Citizen*; ILO (1995c), *Invisible Workers in Viet Nam*; ILO (1992), *Homeworkers of South East Asia (Thailand, Indonesia and Philippines)*.

3.5 Moving the urban informal sector into mainstream development

76.   The potential of the urban informal sector to create new and better jobs is a powerful tool in the hands of local authorities. Whereas it is true that the urban informal sector is often seen as a cushion for the vulnerable and marginalized urban poor, the productive capacity of this sector is often underestimated. Also, while there may be trade-offs between creating new sources of employment and protecting working conditions for those who are already working, improving working conditions in the informal sector can go hand-in-hand with increased productivity and incomes.[39] Investments in health, education and upgrading informal settlements can be very good investments from a purely economic perspective. Therefore, municipal officials should compare more often the potential for employment creation of large-scale industries with that of small and micro-enterprises.

77.   Policies in most developing countries have contributed to a process of marginalization of the informal sector. The policy framework in these countries has often been biased in favour of modern and large firms and against the informal sector, the bias being derived partly from the developmental strategies pursued, e.g., import substitution. However, in the context of globalization, it is more difficult for national governments to protect their formal sector industries; and new opportunities arise for small formal and informal sector enterprises to tie into world markets. In such cases, both national and local governments have a responsibility to see that basic labour standards are respected.

78.   In the past most governments in developing countries viewed the informal sector only as a safety net providing low-productivity employment and hence emphasized its role in poverty alleviation. The sector has been treated as a special target group rather than attempting to integrate it with the mainstream economy, and there has been a neglect of its growth potential. Instead of seeing the low quality of output as something that needs to be overcome, it is often used as a basis for condemning the sector. Added to that, informal sector workers are often treated as belonging to the parallel or underground economy, violating existing regulations. Many countries have revised their attitudes about this sector; some have legally recognized it and its positive contribution, and others have grudgingly accepted its existence. Some have even created new support institutions to assist the sector.

[39]   Bowles and Gintis (1995) show that cross-country data reveal no trade-off between the level of income inequality and the rates of investment or productivity growth across nations. Countries with more equal distributions of income appear, if anything, to perform better on standard macroeconomic measures. The authors suggest that what is required is a change in the structure of economic governance, namely the institutions, norms and conventions that regulate the incentives and constraints faced by economic actors so that both equality and higher productivity are attained.

Box 7:   ***Building networks – an experiment in providing support
to small urban producers in the informal economy***

The main difficulties confronting small urban producers are their isolation, dispersion and lack of organization. This often prevents them from getting beyond the subsistence level to achieve economic security. In 1988, the ILO launched in Benin a Small Urban Producers Programme (SUPP) to overcome these obstacles by organizing group-based networks of employers, employees and apprentices to manage economic and financial services. SUPP is based upon the experience gained from an initial experiment carried out in 15 towns in Mali, Rwanda and Togo, between 1982 and 1989.

Four components are brought together by SUPP: a financial instrument (mutual savings and loan association), a technical, product and production promotion instrument (common facilities workshop), a marketing strategy (market development and diversification) and the promotion of independent socio-occupational federations (as a new social actor). The first mutual and savings loan association in Benin was established in July 1988. Since then 60 have been set up and some of them have merged. They comprise some 1,600 micro-enterprises, employing approximately 6,500 people. Three common facilities workshops have been built and are fully operational; a fourth was (in 1995) under construction.

SUPP is based upon the principles of participatory development. In the first stage, the objective is to get small producers to participate in all aspects of decision-making and planning. In the second stage, it is expected that small producers will begin to develop group strategies and establish flexible networks and support structures. The aim in the long run is to foster the emergence of a credible and self-reliant social actor, capable of engaging in dialogue with the country's institutions. In this context, the State has an important part to play as it must provide economic policy incentives, including marketing outlets, while allowing small producers ample scope for initiative and self-organization.

SUPP and the Government of Benin have taken steps to implement the following reforms:

- amending the investment codes to make it easier for micro-enterprises to start up;
- reforming the tax system by instituting a single tax;
- revising the conditions that enterprises must meet to qualify and bid for public works contracts and other government contracts; and
- calling upon funding agencies and banks to cooperate in opening a credit line to finance rapidly accessible loans.

Source: Maldonado, C. (1993), "Building networks: An experiment in support to small urban producers in Benin", in *International Labour Review*, Vol. 132, No. 2.

79.   Often the existence of a policy bias in favour of the formal sector (much of which actually belongs to the government in certain countries) is attributed to the presence of a lobby; and conversely the bias against the informal sector is explained in terms of the absence of such a lobby. One of the most effective ways to bring about a change in the policy environment may be to encourage the formation of organizations within the informal sector, whether an association of the self-employed or micro-enterprises, a chamber of commerce or a trade association, or a workers' cooperative or organization. Since such associations are generally absent – which is one of the characteristics of the sector – or are fragmented and weak if they exist at all, they should be strengthened to be able to exert pressure on policy-makers, thereby reducing bias. Given the difficulties inherent in implementing labour standards (for example, abolition of child labour, provision of safe and healthy working conditions) in the informal sector, associations, developed from within, may represent one of the most effective means of gradually extending social protection to this sector. Formal sector workers' organizations could join hands with the informal sector to help them organize such associations.

80.   Since the early 1980s, development agencies have designed and supported micro-enterprise development projects aimed at improving access to various resources including credit, technology, skills and inputs with a view to strengthening their technological and production capacity; these had been identified as the main constraints. However, they encountered a number of problems and consequently had to widen their scope and objectives to include the development of a "delivery mechanism" which involved: resource mobilization from within the sector; strengthening the self-management capacity of micro-enterprises; and convincing the authorities to modify the regulatory environment. The following examines how interventions in a number of urban areas can enhance the overall efficiency of the informal sector.

Providing equal access

81.   Micro-enterprises in the informal sector operate under severe resource constraints. Not only do the owners/operators of these enterprises possess little schooling, skills and capital; more important, they are unable to improve their initial endowments and enhance their production capacity as they **lack access** to key inputs and other resources such as land, credit, technical know-how, information and infrastructure, in part as a result of restrictive regulations which have contributed to their marginalization within the urban economy. Full compliance with all regulations is costly and hence regulations have often acted as barriers to integration with the mainstream economy.

82.   One of the key areas in which policy-makers can act is to improve the accessibility of micro-enterprises, which have the potential for creating employment, to resources and services that are already available to others. Although resources are limited, the informal sector, as well as small and medium-sized enterprises in the formal sector, should be at least given the possibility of competing for these limited resources.

83.   The informal sector usually has **unequal access to basic services and infrastructure** which makes it difficult for it to compete on an equal footing with the small-scale formal sector. As already seen, the poor operating out of informal settlements may actually pay more for water supply, housing, transportation, waste removal, etc. than do formal sector enterprises. Also, the lack of certain basic infrastructure such as access roads and drainage increases the cost of doing business out of informal settlements.

84.   Biases against the informal sector have often led to restrictions on its **access to certain markets**, e.g., excluding the involvement of informal enterprises in the development of housing and urban infrastructure, restricting the access of informal transport operators. It is paradoxical that the informal sector is gaining new access to international markets through globalization while its access to local markets continues to be restricted.

85.   Most informal sector enterprises, by definition, do not have a fixed location or proper premises to conduct business and often occupy land over which they have no rights. Despite the rapid growth of the sector, the proportion of land allocated to it has been diminishing.[40] In Manila, one third of the population are squatters in slum areas that occupy less than 5% of the land of the metropolis.[41] The **lack of secure access to land** and premises can also be a widespread problem for small and medium-sized enterprises (SMEs). Access to land is likely to worsen for the urban poor, as city densities begin to increase and more available land is taken up. The built-up area of cities in the developing world is expected to increase by 118% between 1980 and the year 2000.[42] This is almost four times as high as the rate in the cities of the industrialized countries. Without a clear title to land, small and micro-entrepreneurs will have no incentive to improve their premises nor will they be able to get access to credit and other assistance.

[40] UNDP (1994), Issues Paper for Panel on Urban Poverty and Productive Employment, International Colloquium of Mayors on Social Development (New York, 18-19 August 1994).

[41] Zablan, A. (1990), *Vital Issues of the Urban Poor*, Ateneo de Manila, Manila.

[42] Ministry of Foreign Affairs (1994), *Urban Poverty Alleviation*, Ministry of Foreign Affairs, The Netherlands.

86.   If the long-term objective of municipalities is to see the informal sector fully integrated within the urban economy, there clearly must be some policy response. There are a number of steps that municipalities can take to improve access to and increase supply of urban land:

- **reform discriminatory legislation** so that greater protection is provided to the urban landless. For instance, improve rights of tenure, simplify land title procedures and ensure that the application of regulations is equitable and transparent;

- **develop low-cost schemes**, such as covered public markets and workshops, for renting or owner-occupation. This is usually best done in conjunction with the private sector;

- ensure that some of the **development value** generated by urban infrastructure improvement is **used to benefit the local community** that may otherwise be marginalized by the process;

- try to **decentralize and democratize land-use policy and infrastructure decisions**. Neighbourhood groups of small business owners should be viewed as a critical resource in setting infrastructure priorities, since they have the best market information on the bottlenecks to further growth.

87.   In addition to land, the urban poor usually have limited **access to credit**. For the growing number of micro-enterprises in the urban informal sector, the lack of credit restricts their ability to expand or even make marginal improvements in productivity and income. Considerable research and operational projects have highlighted the failure of mainstream financial institutions to serve poor communities. Commercial bank lending procedures are usually too complex and cumbersome, have terms that cannot be complied with and are generally ill-adapted to the nature and capital needs of micro-economic activities. As a result a variety of credit schemes and programmes have emerged that cater directly to the needs of the poor. These include community banks, intermediary programmes, parallel credit schemes and many other variations. However, while their strategies and institutional frameworks may differ, they are united by a central focus on development and poverty alleviation.

88.   **Access of poor women to credit is usually more restricted than that of men**. Facing substantial social, cultural and legal obstacles to credit, poor women have relied heavily on informal sources of credit, such as from family and friends, traditional moneylenders and pawnbrokers. They are thus especially vulnerable to extortionate terms. Box 8 provides an example of a bank that grew out of a women's self-help movement.

Box 8:   **The SEWA Bank in India**

Originating among the women's group of the Textile Labour Association in Ahmedabad in 1972, the Self-Employed Women's Association (SEWA) Union went beyond conventional trades unionism to reach out to self-employed women in urban and rural areas. It is one of the few organizations that consists of, and is targeted at, poor women.

Initially SEWA acted as a go-between for borrowers and national banks. However, due to the difficulties with the established banking system, SEWA members decided to set up their own bank which was registered as a cooperative. The SEWA Bank provides loans for productive purposes, such as tools for a trade, working capital, housing, storage or work space. By 1989, the SEWA Bank had over 11,000 shareholders and had extended over 6,000 loans to its members. Apart from lending, SEWA savings mobilizers visit women at their homes or workplace, weaving their visits into women's work schedules, so that savings can be easily deposited. Close supervision, self-monitoring through participatory processes and building collective consciousness and cooperative values are among the key elements of its success.

Sources: Rose, K. (1992), *Where Women are Leaders: The SEWA Movement in India*, Zed Books, London and New Jersey; UN (1993), *State of Urbanization in Asia and the Pacific*, New York.

89.   Contrary to widespread belief, the poor are creditworthy and have a capacity to save. The Bank Rakyat Indonesia (BRI) developed a system to cater specifically for the poor, which lends at rates that are higher than commercial rates of interest.[43] This corroborates with evaluations of ILO pilot projects which indicate that interest rates do not always have to be subsidized.[44] This is not surprising. Indeed, it is the basic premise of informal sector moneylenders, who usually charge the poor astronomical rates and still make a profit. One of the most promising strategies to create jobs in urban areas is therefore to create or strengthen financial institutions that are particularly adapted to dealing with artisans, the self-employed and small enterprises.

90.   The above arguments point to the economic viability of the urban informal sector. Whereas the second part of this paper raised the gloomy picture of jobless growth, policies to invest in the informal sector can provide hope for **employment-intensive growth**. This strategy means moving beyond the traditional concept of support to the informal sector as a social safety net to catch those who fall from mainstream economic development. For better or worse, the urban informal sector, in developing transitional and industrialized country cities, *is* already a strong component of mainstream development. Local officials can use its potential to create and safeguard employment.

91.   The principal asset of a poor person is his or her labour.[45] Increasing the productivity of this asset through improvements in training is one of the keys to employability, raising earnings and reducing inequality in income distribution.[46] Training and education enhance an individual's capacity to respond to market opportunities and provide a route to more skilled and better paying jobs.[47] The unemployed and underemployed urban poor do not, however, have easy access to these services. In the first place, poor urban neighbourhoods have fewer and poorer quality schools and health facilities, which provide a foundation for development of human capital. Also, specialized training institutions are often linked to formal sector enterprises (either run by private businesses, or designed to cater for their needs). Workers' and employers' organizations are increasingly realizing that it is in their interests to develop outreach components of their training programmes specifically targeted towards the informal sector.

[43]   BRI is a government-owned and initiated bank. Savings deposited with it grew from US$38 million in 1984 to US$460 million in 1989, representing over 6,600,000 savers with average deposits of US$70.

[44]   ILO (1991c), "The ILO and the financial sector" (consultation report), 19 September 1991, ILO/ENTERPRISE (unpublished), Geneva.

[45]   ILO (1995b), op. cit.

[46]   Ibid.

[47]   Education and training are not necessarily the same thing. Job training programmes have goals that are much more direct than those of education. While the latter generally encompasses moral and intellectual purposes, the former is exclusively focused on preparing individuals for employment.

3.6   The regulatory environment: Implications for job creation and social protection

92.   The regulatory environment is an issue which cuts across investment policies, informal sector development and growth of employment. Local governments have the power to use or abuse regulations with major consequences for employment. In this era of deregulation, it might be fashionable to argue that all government-imposed regulations should be abolished. There are those who believe that to promote the informal sector,

Removing discriminatory regulations

to allow it to make its full contribution to the economy, requires the destruction of regulations. If this was to happen, there would be a constant threat to workers' health and safety. To be sure, there are regulations which do not serve any useful purpose. While there may be trade-offs between two good things, for example environment and employment or safety and employment, such trade-offs should be acknowledged and people should make an explicit democratic choice between the alternatives.

93.   In some cases there is a need for a radical reappraisal of laws and regulations governing business registration and urban planning. Complicated procedures for registering enterprises, strict zoning laws banning businesses from operating in residential areas, harassment by local authorities, a multiplicity of permits and reporting requirements, can all lead to substantial burdens for enterprises in both the formal and informal sectors (see Box 9). It is wrong to assume that informal sector enterprises have no wish to regularize their operations. Sometimes, they remain illegal simply because they cannot afford the cost that is imposed by prolonged bureaucratic processes and multiple legal requirements.

Box 9:   The informal sector – legalization or laissez-faire?

Studies carried out in about 20 countries have assessed the repercussions of regulations on the creation, development and operation of informal sector activities. These studies show that most enterprises in the informal sector are in fact operating on a semi-legal basis. However, while most of them comply with a few basic regulations (including local authorization, registration and licences), very few enterprises observe national tax and labour requirements. Part of the reason for non-compliance lies in the high cost implications.

In an ILO survey of several African countries,* it was found that full compliance with existing legislation would result in a 30% reduction in the monthly earnings of the average informal sector entrepreneur in Benin, Burundi and Tunisia, while in the Central African Republic this would amount to a reduction of 88%. Legalization brings about a number of advantages, such as lower risks of forced closure, fines and confiscation of goods, and improved health, safety and workers' welfare. However, while legalization can facilitate access to credit, public markets and favourable treatment under investment codes, structural factors (e.g., the entrepreneur's solvency, experience and skills, technological level of the enterprise, volume of operations) remain highly important. These studies identified five priority areas for policy reform :

- progressive tax relief measures for informal sector enterprises;
- flexibility in the laws governing employment contracts and wages;
- social security schemes based upon the resources available to the informal sector;
- measures aimed at improving the access of informal sector enterprises to capital and markets;
- reduction in the number and cost of administrative and regulatory procedures.

* Benin, Burundi, Central African Republic and Tunisia.
Source: Maldonado, C. (1995), "The informal sector – legalization or laissez-faire", in *International Labour Review*, Vol. 134, No. 6.

94.   In some cases, urban by-laws may need to be completely revamped since they are either out of date or wholly inappropriate. "It is interesting to note the origins of the Nairobi by-laws. They were just picked from Blackburn (a town in Britain) and used unaltered except for the name which changed from Blackburn to Nairobi".[48] Small labour-intensive enterprises (most of which are in the informal sector) suffer the most since the costs of regulation tend to be fixed and do not vary with size.[49]

[48]   Tournée, J. and Omwanza, J. (1995), op. cit., p. 109.

[49]   World Bank (1991), op. cit.

95.   Governments can lessen the regulatory barriers that are faced by enterprises by:

- streamlining bureaucracy and reducing registration fees to a nominal amount;
- supervising and training law enforcers;
- disseminating information and simplifying requirements; and
- reforming restrictive zoning laws.

96.   All of the above measures are within the competence of local authorities. It is up to them to decide the costs and benefits of each measure in their particular situation. Such measures may actually reduce administration cost and allow funds to be directed to economically and socially more worthwhile areas.

97.   Ignoring labour standards is likely to generate, other things being equal, a higher level of disguised unemployment. What the world needs is not simply more jobs, but higher quality jobs with rising real wages which respect commonly agreed labour standards. This is feasible if there is an increase in the rate of growth of real world demand. A common objection to labour standards is that they cannot be enforced in the informal sector in developing countries. A large proportion of informal sector businesses tend to be small and family-run. There is therefore substance in the argument that the enforcement of labour standards is impractical in this sector of the economy.

Social protection and the applicability of international labour standards

98.   The relationship therefore between the informal sector and international labour standards is a subject fraught with questions. Policy-makers are confronted with the dilemma expressed by ILO Recommendation No.169 on Employment Policy, which encourages the progressive integration of the informal sector into national economies, while recognizing that this integration may reduce the informal sector's ability to absorb labour and generate income. As a general approach, the Report of the Director-General (ILO), 1991, has suggested that the basic standards and provisions of labour legislation should be regarded as goals to be attained progressively in the informal sector – beginning with the more viable enterprises.[50]

[50]   ILO (1991a), GB. 251/CE/5/2, 251st Session, November 1991, para. 28, Geneva.

99.   However, while a progressive approach is clearly a pragmatic and essential requirement for "legalizing" the informal sector, there are a number of fundamental labour standards that should apply to all workers independently of where they work. In other words, the progressive application of labour standards does not, in all cases, have to wait until the informal sector starts to "catch up" with the formal sector. The precarious and unregulated nature of work, in either the informal or formal sector, cannot be regarded as a norm. There are certain core standards that are so fundamental that their non-observance should not be tolerated.

Serge Cid, ILO Geneva

100.   These fundamental standards deal with basic human rights and child labour. Freedom of association (ILO Conventions Nos. 87 and 98), freedom from forced labour (Nos. 29 and 105) and freedom from discrimination (Nos. 100 and 111) are the six basic human rights Conventions that require priority attention. The importance attached to these Conventions is reflected by the fact that well over 100 ILO member States have ratified all of them. As commented by the Director-General of the ILO in 1991: *Practical measures will need to be taken in the countries concerned to ensure that national legislation is fully in accordance with these basic standards, that informal sector workers are made fully aware of their rights and have the possibility of asserting and enjoying them. National organizations of employers and workers should, in particular, be encouraged and assisted in their efforts to ensure that these standards are known, understood and applied in the informal sector.*[51]

51   Ibid.

101.   In some cases, this may actually involve the removal of legal obstacles faced by the informal sector. For instance, in some countries, people working in the informal sector are not recognized by legislation as workers and employers. Without such recognition, they are unable to gain legal authorization to form organizations, gain access to social services or protection from discrimination in employment.

102.   A constructive solution to this problem is to use education and the media to increase awareness in the informal sector of the usefulness of labour standards for people's health and safety, and to show that they are not just good for workers, but also for employers in that they may lead to greater productivity. NGOs may be involved both in the educational task and in advising on methods for compliance with the standards.

103.   There are also other means to extend social protection, apart from legislation. The vulnerability of the poor is caused by a combination of factors, such as the irregularity and low levels of income, the lack of education, the casual, informal and temporary nature of labour arrangements and the lack of access to social insurance schemes. Together with establishing legal rights, programmes are required that will provide basic social security and health care, upgrade the physical working and living environment of the informal sector, provide basic urban services, improve productivity and incomes, and help the self-employed organize and strengthen their bargaining power and become aware of their rights. The application of international labour standards to the informal sector requires a comprehensive strategy that can address all of these issues.

3.7   Forming new alliances

104.   People all over the world are searching for new and creative ways of working together to tackle society's increasingly complex challenges. Building partnerships among employers, workers, different levels of government, NGOs, business and community-based organizations is increasingly seen as the way forward. Over the last 20 years there has been an almost universal policy shift from *the State as a provider* to *the State as an enabler*. Results have been mixed. It is reasonable to expect that private initiatives and more competition in the operation of urban services will improve efficiency and reliability. At the same time, community involvement, particularly of the urban poor, is required to avoid the risk that the poor may be excluded and marginalized. Nevertheless, the private sector plays a vital role in generating jobs, creating wealth and improving services. The challenge for local governments is to forge partnerships with the private sector, and with employers' and workers' organizations, to make them more actively involved in urban development and job creation.

105.   The urban unemployed and poor do not lack initiative, ingenuity, or industriousness. Indeed, an enterprising response is often required to survive in an environment of disadvantage and limited opportunity. The formation of self-help organizations is a vital part of this response. Self-help organizations provide an effective institutional means to improve the employment situation of the urban poor through the following:

Self-help organizations and participatory development for the urban poor

- building institutions that **articulate their interests**, much as trade unions do for formal sector workers;

- providing vital **social services** and crisis support. Often the urban poor do not have access to basic social services. Through collective action, a form of social security is created with members providing mutual support;

- acting as a **channel for assistance**. The creation of an identifiable organization is an important means of forming linkages with local authorities, government agencies, NGOs and other donor agencies. This helps to improve access to training, contracts and financial assistance – thus generating further employment opportunities;

- improving **linkages with the formal sector**. Modern sector enterprises can contribute to economic development and employment by subcontracting both services and some supplies from small informal sector establishments. To maintain the quality and effectiveness of the services, training and assistance to these small enterprises could be provided by the contracting firms. Fiscal incentives could be used to promote this type of scheme. Moreover, by grouping together, the self-employed and small enterprises can negotiate and tender for services in the formal sector in a competitive manner;

- providing a **catalyst for community-based upgrading**, including articulation of community priorities, execution of works through community contracts and collecting community contributions for operation and maintenance.

Box 10: **Community-based upgrading – the Kalerwe Project, Uganda and Hanna Nassif, United Republic of Tanzania**

Kalerwe, an informal settlement in Kampala, is a low-lying area prone to flooding during the rainy seasons. The improvement of the drainage system was a high priority for residents. Community contracts were used to ensure that the residents played a leading role in the identification, planning and subsequent implementation of the project activities. The Kampala City Council, the Ministry of Finance and Economic Planning and of Lands, Housing and Urban Development were also actively involved. Apart from the immediate technical objectives, the pilot project sought:

- to create the capacity of public authorities to undertake an enabling approach to infrastructure upgrading; and
- to develop and test the capacity of the community contracting system.

Rapid progress was made in completing the main drain and the majority of the secondary drains. In total, 14,307 workdays were generated for skilled and unskilled labour. This amounted to an average of work for 60 people per day. However, the impact of the project should be evaluated not just in terms of the quantity of jobs created. Social, economic and health surveys indicate a reduction in the prevalence of water-borne diseases, increased variety of economic activities in the area and greater construction activity. Although progress during construction was rapid, the drainage network is now facing maintenance problems which will have to be resolved with both the Kampala City Council and community residents.

In Hanna Nassif, one of the 44 unplanned settlements in Dar-es-Salaam with similar problems of flooding, more is expected from the community. The Hanna Nassif Community Development Committee has financial control and is responsible for all procurement and letting of small contracts to artisans. However, there are a number of difficulties due to conflicts within the community and insufficient managerial capacity. Also, despite commitments, the level of community contributions has been lower than expected. Construction is now under way but progress has been slow. As a pilot project, Hanna Nassif highlighted many of the difficulties of dealing directly with communities, relying on support from city council staff and using communities to implement technically demanding works. The community contracting system is still undergoing changes to reflect these important lessons.

The Kalerwe and Hanna Nassif projects nevertheless illustrate the feasibility of community-based upgrading, an area often overlooked by investment planners.

Sources: ILO (1994b), "Kalerwe community-based drainage upgrading project (In-depth evaluation report)", and ILO (1995a), "Draft workshop proceedings on the National Seminar on Investment Policies for Employment and Poverty Alleviation" (ILO/Government of Uganda), 9-11 May 1995, Entebbe, Uganda.

106.   A number of measures can be taken, in partnership with trade unions, employers' organizations, NGOs and international agencies to promote self-help associations. These include the following:

- **creating a favourable legislative and policy framework.** The protection of the rights of cooperatives and other self-help organizations should be on equal terms with other enterprises;

- building partnerships with cooperatives and other self-help associations. There are a number of successful instances of **trade unions taking the initiative** to promote cooperatives. For instance, in India, a trade union encouraged its members to organize themselves into a workers' cooperative and take over the ownership and management of an industrial enterprise that had been in a poor condition for several years. Within one year, the company was revived and has since been made into a profitable enterprise, thereby maintaining many jobs. Also in India, trade unions have sponsored the formation of consumer, savings and credit, and housing cooperatives;

- **channelling financial support** in the form of loans, credit guarantees, grants and/or tax reductions or exemptions through the self-help movement, provided that it is capable of assuming responsibility for its use and/or repayment. Emphasis should be given to supporting activities that can clearly demonstrate how the funds can be used to create employment and improve income levels;

- meeting **training and development needs**. The emphasis should be on providing practical skills that can be readily used to solve pressing problems. Not all self-help associations will require the same type or level of skills development. Initially, areas where training could improve the operation of the organization should be assessed. In addition, care should be taken that appropriate methods and media are used for disseminating information. There is no point in developing training packages that cannot be used by the target audience.

107.   An appropriate institutional framework is critical to ensuring the effectiveness and sustainability of new alliances. The promotion of local development networks with many stakeholders is one of the key steps in forming such a framework. These networks help create a pool of expertise with each partner providing a specific type of contribution (see Box 11). For instance, formal sector workers can help unorganized labour by providing education, training and advice on a range of labour issues. The government, both national and local, through its various agencies can gather information, provide guidelines, raise awareness of working conditions and help create an appropriate regulatory environment. The private sector has a key role to play in generating access to new markets, improving productivity, transferring managerial and other business skills, and in assisting with product development and technological innovation. The non-governmental sector can provide the entry point for working at grassroots level and help raise levels of community participation. These local economic development networks should act as both a forum and partnership agency for formulating and implementing creative and market-led initiatives for productive and sustainable employment.

Box 11: **The value of partnership**

Cooperation between diverse groups has many advantages:

- it can mobilize greater amounts and a wider variety of skills and resources than can be achieved by acting alone;
- it can address problems in a more integrated multidisciplinary and comprehensive manner;
- it can eliminate unnecessary duplication of cost and effort, which is especially important where there are shortages of financial resources or relevant skills;
- it can help traditional adversaries, or organizations which have had little cause to interact in the past, to broaden their perspectives and to respect each others' needs and capabilities;
- this in turn can facilitate the dialogue, creativity and mutual trust needed to work through diverse and apparently conflicting interests, towards common goals;
- the multiple face-to-face interaction which occurs between partners can also facilitate the flow of information and promote technology transfer.

Source: UNEP and The Prince of Wales Business Leaders Forum (1994), *Partnerships for Sustainable Development: The Role of Business and Industry*, London.

Public-private partnerships

108.   Commerce and industry have a critical role to play in the future of employment, given their potential for generating new jobs, new markets, products and services. There is general consensus that small and medium-sized enterprises (SMEs – both formal and informal) account for 60% to 90% of overall employment. The importance of SMEs for generating employment is likely to increase since:

- in the vast majority of developing countries the economy consists more and more of SMEs, with big companies increasingly breaking themselves into networks of small, relatively independent units;
- in industrialized countries local governments are increasingly privatizing municipal services in such areas as refuse collection and recycling, infrastructural maintenance functions, water supply, sewerage and health provision;
- in industrialized countries large enterprises continue to outsource their activities to SMEs;
- in general, SMEs are increasingly successful in adapting to the challenges of economic globalization. This includes SMEs both in inner cities of industrialized countries and in urban areas of developing countries.

However, SMEs face a number of constraints similar to those confronted by micro-enterprises in the informal sector. By working with the business community to reduce these constraints, municipal governments can use SMEs as another tool at their disposal for employment creation.

109.   One of the important areas in which the private sector can be directed to contribute to local economic development is in training (see Box 12). This is particularly so given the rapid changes taking place in the world of work. Public-private partnerships in training can help mobilize a collective effort to ensure an optimum response to the skill development needs of individuals and enterprises in an environment of rapid change.

Large private enterprises should also be encouraged within the framework of public-private partnerships to develop links with SMEs. This can be done by developing financial incentives for subcontracting to small suppliers, establishing subcontracting exchanges and by setting criteria for likely contributions to local supplier networks when assessing inward investment proposals.

Box 12: Public-private partnerships for training

In Chile, where there is a tradition of highly centralized government, the reforms in the early 1980s included significant decentralization, which resulted in the creation by local entrepreneurs and the public authorities of four Regional Councils for Education and Work (CRET). This employer-led initiative exemplifies the growing role of the private sector in Chile and the importance of local action in the field of technical and vocational education and training. CRETs are designed to promote efficiency, quality and labour market relevance of technical and vocational training through greater enterprise participation in policy formulation, curricula design, teacher training, financing, coordination and the pooling of resources. They also represent local interests in negotiations with the central government on policy issues.

Source: Mitchell, A. (1995), "Strategic training partnerships between the State and enterprises", Discussion Paper, ILO Training Policies Branch, Geneva.

---

110. Cooperation among SMEs can also be an important vehicle for improving competitiveness and productivity. Notwithstanding the competitive environment in which private sector enterprises work, collective arrangements can provide a way to compensate for individual resource weaknesses and help SMEs develop technical know-how, use economies of scale and improve their capacity to switch production processes and products with greater efficiency. This enhances the scope of an enterprise to tackle new kinds of work. Inter-firm cooperation in small groups, say of five or six enterprises, or larger groups, may be used to address a common need (such as credit or access to specialized information) which can in turn lead to other forms of cooperation.

111. In developed countries, a number of experiments have been undertaken to harness the potential of the private sector to regenerate inner-city areas with conditions on a level with those in cities of the developing world. In the UK, where the experiments have been the most market-oriented, a host of initiatives were created in the 1980s. Most notable of these experiments was the creation of urban development corporations to foster public-private partnerships, enterprise zones with tax incentives and no planning restrictions, simplified planning zones, city action task forces and business in the community schemes. The results from these experiments have been mixed. The cost of pump-priming private sector developments has not always been matched by benefits to

inner-city communities. In many cases, the types of jobs that were created were just not suited to the skills of the target group. Those that benefited included people who neither belonged to the area nor were the most disadvantaged. This is not to say that public-private partnerships cannot work, but that greater attention to evaluating projects in terms of their direct impact on the target community is required.

112.   Nevertheless, there are some positive lessons that can be drawn from the experiments taken in the inner cities of developed countries. First, outsourcing by established private sector firms to SMEs in inner city areas can create additional employment. New, inner-city enterprises can be just as price-competitive and efficient as more established firms. Second, contrary to popular perception, the experiments demonstrated that local governments are actually the best agent for promoting public-private partnerships. Greater financial resources and authority should thus be decentralized to local governments. Third, governments are themselves major buyers of a wide range of goods and services. However, this tends to be targeted at a particular segment of the private sector – usually the larger, more established firms. Municipalities could just as easily subcontract services such as garbage collection, recycling and park maintenance from SMEs. However, privatization may not offer a solution to all problems. Fourth, the potential of public-private partnerships in local economic development depends to a large extent on the capacity of both the private and public sector within a country. Policies to promote public-private partnerships also have to take full account of the diversity between sectors, industries and geographical regions.

Box 13:   *The Dublin Inner-City Partnership*

The Dublin Inner-City Partnership Company was launched in 1991 under the Irish Programme for Economic and Social Progress. Trade unions, employers, and construction and farming organizations combined with government agencies to combat problems associated with long-term unemployment. The main aim was to improve the skills and confidence of the long-term unemployed by increasing their involvement in the community while enhancing their employment opportunities through local economic projects. The initiative takes a holistic approach, addressing the full array of problems faced by the long-term unemployed. Local people are encouraged to set up enterprises and employers are persuaded not to discriminate against the long-term unemployed in their recruitment selection procedures. A programme of action has been devised. Tasks include small business expansion and relocation support, and improved access to education and training. The key achievement of the Partnership has been the furthering of working relationships among community groups, the local authority and employers.

Source: EC (1994), *Urban Innovation and Employment Generation*, Brussels.

3.8 Developing capacity and mobilizing resources

113.   All of the policy prescriptions which have been outlined in part 3 of this paper have implications for both capacity development and resource mobilization at the municipal level. Whereas municipal governments are the first to feel the pressure caused by unemployment, they are more used to managing the crisis than to trying to solve it. Trying to solve it will require developing new types of capacity at the municipal level better adapted to both decentralized (from the national to the local level) responsibilities and a globalized economy. It is worthwhile briefly recalling just a few illustrative examples of the new types of knowledge and capacity that will be required for employment creation at the municipal level since without these, there is little hope of putting the policies into practice.

Capacity development

- Employment-intensive investment policies require knowledge, among municipal technical services, of how to manage a different mix of labour and equipment, and of how to tender works out to small-scale, and at times, informal sector contractors. Municipalities will also have to develop an economic analytical capacity to evaluate investment plans to increase their impact on employment creation and on informal sector development.

- To take advantage of potential opportunities offered by globalization, and to better fend off the shocks, municipalities will have to develop both economic and commercial capacities that were previously the domain of national governments. Municipal "commercial attachés" will need to be trained to identify new market opportunities for which a given municipality may have a comparative advantage, and to recommend the priority infrastructure investments required to attract new outside investors. Economic advisors will have to speak out in international policy fora and warn the politicians on how best to prepare for major shifts in the international economy.

- Special knowledge will be required to move from the traditional role of provider, to that of enabler. In particular, municipal officials may require training to learn how to deal with the urban informal sector and to enhance its potential for employment creation, rather than simply to regard it as something to be ignored or banned.

Resource mobilization

114.   Developing the capacities to implement new policies requires resources. To a certain extent, employment creation will pay for itself and help pay for other badly needed municipal investments and services, by creating the necessary tax base. Also, there may be scope for carrying out employment-intensive investments by reprioritizing and by shifting existing investment resources from capital-intensive to labour-intensive approaches.

115.   However, creating employment will require new sources and strategies for resource mobilization. National and local government planners alike should recognize not just the costs associated with creating employment, but also the costs of sustaining high levels of unemployment if the required resources are not allocated. Under decentralization, central governments may recognize that job creation is in the best interest of all parties, and that unemployment can be efficiently addressed at the local level. Therefore, national governments will need to ensure that necessary resources are decentralized together with new responsibilities, and that local governments are authorized to raise their own funds, on local and international financial markets, or to directly approach the donor community.

116.   The international development community is likewise recognizing that prioritizing international development assistance towards the rural sector will not solve the urban crisis. Domestic employment creation is a policy tool for addressing the sensitive problem of international migration. Unemployment, like environmental degradation, is now a global problem requiring global solutions which will have to be implemented increasingly in urban areas at the level of city governments. Therefore, the donor community may review its assistance policies, in order to give greater emphasis to the impact of this assistance on urban employment creation. It may be possible, in particular, to support new urban employment creation and poverty alleviation initiatives, such as the Urban Poverty Partnership being developed by the ILO in collaboration with other international agencies.

4. CONCLUSION: WHAT IS THE FUTURE OF URBAN EMPLOYMENT?

Fabio Decorato

117.   This paper has provided an overview of the impact that current economic, demographic and social trends are having on the level and structure of urban employment. Continued urban population growth, technological change, informalization of work, rising levels of poverty, and the globalization of markets and production systems raise many new challenges for employment policy:

- How will work be organized and employment structured in the coming century, when over half of the world's population will be living in cities?

- With globalization and new production and information technologies leading to increases in productivity, will the world also increasingly be divided between the employed and the unemployed, between those with good jobs and those with bad jobs, between the productive and the unproductive?

- If full employment cannot be assumed in the future, what methods of income distribution can be devised to ensure social and political stability?

118.   The purpose of this paper has not been to provide all the answers or prescriptions, but rather to stimulate discussion on the intertwined future of urban employment and the economy. In conclusion, it is useful to highlight some of the key issues that were debated during the Habitat II Dialogue on The Future of Urban Employment. Since the Dialogue was part of a global conference, these issues are relevant for all areas of the world. They are also issues where a tripartite perspective can provide a unique vantage point and, possibly, new solutions.

119.   The first issue is the **impact of technological change** on job creation, employment structures and the location of industries and services. Technological change with the introduction of more labour-saving production methods has heightened fears of "jobless growth". Computer-based and telecommunications-related processes are revolutionizing virtually all sectors and are transforming both employment structures and the patterns of work. Rapid advancement in information and communications technology are increasingly reducing the importance of geographical distance. This calls into question the assumed advantages of urban agglomeration economies. Even in the sphere of agriculture, the spread of biotechnology is likely to result in important future employment impacts. Employment changes in agriculture are in turn likely to impact upon rural-urban linkages and migration systems. According to historical experience, major technological revolutions create far more jobs than they destroy. If this is the case, is there any need to be concerned about the changes that are now taking place? Can we be confident that current unemployment problems are transitory?

120.   The second issue is the **role and capacity of local, national and international institutions in a global economy**. At the national and international levels, new legal, social and macro-economic policies and means of action which are conducive to employment-oriented growth need to be developed. At the national level, micro-economic reform will be required to improve the efficiency of labour and capital markets. Improvements in sectoral policies, regional development programmes and other direct target interventions are also required. At the local level, it is necessary to reorient investments in favour of employment, to create an enabling regulatory environment and to forge new alliances. While employment policies usually operate within a national framework, there is increasingly a need to establish a cooperative international framework given the global nature and interconnectedness of the problems faced. What new structures are required to develop and implement employment-oriented economic policies? What should be the content and scope of these policies? Are market mechanisms sufficient by themselves to generate productive employment? What impact will globalization have on labour standards, wages and skills? Can or should governments seek to control global market forces?

121.   The third issue is that of the **informalization of work**. The growth of the urban informal sector is relevant to industrial, transitional and developing economies. Almost all countries in the world are facing the threat of precarious, unprotected work and the growth of the informal economy which functions – and often poorly – as a de facto social safety net, rather than a source of productive, appropriately remunerated and freely chosen employment. There has also been a growing trend towards temporary and part-time jobs. Globalization of production has led to growth in subcontracting and the use of casual and contract workers with no job and social security provisions. Will continued globalization lead to further informalization of work, or will it provide a bridge for integration with the formal economy? What impact will continued informalization have on economic growth? In one scenario, it is postulated that the lack of job security, alongside part-time work and widened income inequalities, serves to undermine consumer confidence and if left unchecked will lead to a downward demand spiral – making sustained economic recovery that much harder to achieve. Given the growth of unorganized labour, what will be the role of trade unions in the twenty-first century? Is trade unionism more relevant than ever or is it an outdated concept of the industrial era? What new forms of workers' organizations can be envisaged for the twenty-first century and will trade unions be at the vanguard of these changes?

122.   These are revolutionary times in the world of work. The challenges to finding a global solution to the problems of unemployment are great but they are not beyond us. The Second United Nations Conference on Human Settlements and the Habitat II Dialogue on the Future of Urban Employment, by bringing together a diversity of actors and viewpoints, provided an opportunity for contributing to a global vision of employment into the twenty-first century, an opportunity for taking control of our common destiny and to strive for a more equitable and prosperous future.

Bibliography

- Bairoch, P. 1983. "Tendances et caractéristiques de l'urbanisation du Tiers Monde d'avant-hier à après demain (1900-2005)", in *Revue du Tiers Monde*, avril-juin, Paris.

- Bowles, S. and Gintis, H. 1995. "Productivity-enhancing egalitarian policies", in *International Labour Review*, Vol. 134, No. 4-5.

- Caplowitz, D. 1967. *The Poor Pay More*, Free Press, New York.

- Cohen, M.A. 1976. "Cities in developing countries: 1975-2000", in *Finance and Development*, March issue.

- Collier, P. 1988. "Oil shocks and food security in Nigeria", in *International Labour Review*, Vol. 127, No. 6.

- De Janvry, A., et al. 1995. *Poverty and Rural Labour in South Asia, Latin America and sub-Saharan Africa*, University of California, Berkely.

- De Soto, Hernando. 1989. *The Other Path: The Invisible Revolution in the Third World*, Harper and Row, New York.

- Dornbusch, R. 1985. "Policy and performance links between LDC debtors and industrial nations", in *Brookings Papers on Economic Activity*, Vol. 2.

- Economic Commission (EC). 1994. *Urban Innovation and Employment Generation*, Brussels.

- Eatwell. 1995. "Disguised unemployment: G7 experience", a lecture delivered at South Bank University, London.

- *The Economist*. 1995. "A Survey of Cities", July 29th-August 4th issue.

- Fass, S.M. 1977. "Families in Port-au-Prince: A study of the economics of survival", USAID, Washington, D.C.

- Freeman, C. 1989. "New technology and catching up", in *European Journal of Economic Development*, Vol. 1, No. 1.

- Gaude, J. and Miller, S. (eds.). 1992. "Productive employment for the poor", in a special issue of *International Labour Review*, Vol. 131, No. 1.

- Harpman, T., et al. 1988. *In the Shadow of the City: Community Health and the Urban Poor*, Oxford University Press, Oxford.

- Hardoy, J. and Satterthwaite, D. 1995. *Squatter Citizens*, Earthscan Publications Ltd., London.

- Imschoot, Marc van. 1993. "Burkina Faso. Note sur les modalités de mise en place de la composante HIMO du PASECT du projet d'assistance PNUD/BIT – BKF/87/011, avril 1993".

- International Labour Office (ILO). 1976. *Employment, Growth and Basic Needs: A World Problem*, Geneva.

- ——. 1991a. GB 251/CE/S/2, 251st Session, November 1991, Geneva.

- ——. 1991b. *Summaries of International Labour Standards*, Second Edition, Geneva.

- ——. 1991c. "The ILO and the financial sector" (consultation report), 19 September, ILO/ENTERPRISE (unpublished), Geneva.

- ——. 1992a. *Homeworkers of South-East Asia (Thailand, Indonesia and the Philippines)*, Geneva.

- ——. 1992b. *World Labour Report 1992*, Geneva.

- ——. 1994a. "Politiques d'investissement et utilisation intensive des ressources locales: Perspectives pour la création d'emplois et l'économie de devises dans les pays de la zone CFA" (Rapport Provisoire), septembre 1994, Genève.

- ——. 1994b. "Kalerwe community-based drainage upgrading project (In-depth evaluation report)", Geneva.

- ——. 1995a. Draft workshop proceedings on the National Seminar on Investments Policies for Employment Generation and Poverty Alleviation (ILO/Government of Uganda), 9-11 May 1995, Entebbe, Uganda.

- ——. 1995b. *Gender, Poverty and Employment: Turning Capabilities into Entitlements*, Geneva.

- ——. 1995c. *Invisible Workers in Viet Nam*, Geneva.

- ——. 1995d. *World Employment Report 1995*, Geneva.

- ——. 1995e. *From Want to Work*, Geneva.

- ——. 1995f. *The Employment Challenge in Latin America and the Caribbean*, Working Paper No. 7, Lima.

- ——. 1995g. *World Labour Report 1995*, Geneva.

- ——. 1996. *World Employment Report 1996/97*, Geneva.

- International Monetary Fund (IMF). 1997. *World Economic Outlook*, October issue.

- Krugman, P. 1995. "Urban concentration: The role of increasing returns and transport costs", Proceedings of the World Bank Annual Conference on Development Economics.

- Lee, E. 1995. "Overview of the special issue: Employment policy in the global economy", in *International Labour Review*, Vol. 134, No. 4-5.

- Lewis, W.A. 1978. *The Evolution of the International Economic Order*, Princeton University Press, Princeton.

- Liu, J. C. 1993. "Growth of employment in the informal sector in China: A review", ILO, Geneva (unpublished document).

- Maldonado, C. 1993. "Building networks: An experiment in support to small urban producers in Benin", in *International Labour Review*, Vol. 132, No. 2.

- ——. 1995. "The informal sector: Legalization or laissez-faire", in *International Labour Review*, Vol. 134, No. 6.

- Mazo, S., et al. 1986. "Shelter strategies for the urban poor in developing countries", in *World Bank Research Observer*.

- Ministry of Foreign Affairs, The Netherlands. 1994. *Urban Poverty Alleviation*, The Hague.

- Mitchell, A. 1995. "Strategic training partnerships between the State and enterprises", Discussion Paper, ILO Training Policies Branch, Geneva.

- National Commission on Urbanization, Government of India. *Interim Report 1988*. New Delhi.

- Nielsen, E. Vang. 1992. "Policy paper for the local resource-based approach (Labour-based construction)", African Development Bank, Abidjan (draft).

- Oberai, A.S. 1993. *Population Growth, Employment and Poverty in Third-World Mega-Cities – Analytical and Policy Issues*, St. Martin's Press Inc., New York.

- Olpadwala, P. and Goldsmith, W.W. 1992. "The sustainability of privilege: Reflections on the environment, the Third World city and poverty", in *World Development*, Vol. 20, No. 4.

- Perlman, J. 1986. "Six misconceptions about squatter settlements", in *Development*, Vol. 4.

- ——. 1990. "Global urbanization and the transfer of innovations", Workshop in Urbanization, Migration and Economic Development, U.S. National Academy of Sciences, Washington, D.C.

- Rodgers, G. 1989. *Urban Poverty and the Labour Market: Access to Jobs and Incomes in Asian and Latin American Cities*, ILO, Geneva.

- Rogers, R. 1995. "The BBC Reith Lectures", in *The Independent*, published from 13 February to 13 March.

- Rose, K. 1992. *Where Women are Leaders: The SEWA Movement in India*, Zed Books, London and New Jersey.

- Rowthorn, R.E. and Wells, J. 1987. *De-Industrialization and Foreign Trade*, Cambridge University Press, Cambridge.

- Sachs, C. 1986. "Multirao in Brazil – Initiatives for self-reliance", in *Development*, Vol. 4.

- Sachs, I. 1986. "Work, food and energy in urban ecodevelopment", in *Development*, Vol. 4.

- Sassen, S. 1991. *The Global City*, Princeton University Press, Princeton.

- Sethuraman, S.V. 1997. "Urban poverty and the informal sector: A critical assessment of current strategies", draft, ILO/UNDP.

- Simai, M. 1995. *Global Employment: An International Investigation into the Future of Work*, Zed Books, London and New Jersey.

- Singh, A. 1979. "The basic needs approach to development versus the new international economic order: The significance of third world industrialisation", in *World Development*, June.

- ——. 1987. "Manufacturing and de-industrialization", in *The New Palgrave: A Dictionary of Economics*, Macmillan, London.

- ——. 1989. "Third World competition and de-industrialisation in advanced countries", In *CJE*, Vol. 13.

- ——. 1992a. "The actual crisis of economic development in the 1980s: An alternative policy perspective for the future", in A. Dutt and K. Jameson (eds.): *New Directions in Development Economics*, Edward Elgar, Aldershot, UK.

- ——. 1992b. "Urbanization, poverty and employment: The large metropolis in the Third World", in *Contributions to Political Economy*, Vol. 11.

- ——. 1995. "Institutional requirements for full employment in advanced economies", in *International Labour Review*, Vol. 134, No. 4-5.

- —— and Tabatabai, H. 1993. *Economic Crisis and Third World Agriculture*, Cambridge University Press, Cambridge.

- Singla, P.P. 1991. "Programme advisory note on labour-intensive infrastructure and works programme", ILO, Geneva.

- Standing, G. 1995. "Enterprise restructuring in Russian industry and mass unemployment: The RLFS Fourth Round", ILO, Working Paper.

- Tipple, G. 1993. "Shelter as a workplace: A review of home-based enterprise in developing countries", in *International Labour Review*, Vol. 132, No. 4.

- Tournée, J. and Omwanza, J. 1995. "Alternative strategies for the provision of infrastructure in urban unplanned settlements", in *Labour-based Technology – A Review of Current Practice*, Vol. 2, ILO, Geneva.

- United Nations (UN). 1985. *Migration, Population Growth and Employment in Metropolitan Areas of Selected Developing Countries*, New York.

- ——. 1990. *World Economic Survey*, New York.

- ——. 1993. *State of Urbanization in Asia and the Pacific*, New York.

- ——. 1995a. *Migration, Population Growth and Employment in Metropolitan Areas of Selected Developing Countries*, New York.

- ——. 1995b. *World Economic Survey*, New York.

- ——. 1997. *World Urbanization Prospects: The 1996 Revision*, New York.

- UNCED. 1989. "Agenda 21, Chapter 7: Promoting sustainable human settlement development".

- United Nations Centre for Human Settlements (UNCHS)/ILO. 1995. *Shelter Provision and Employment Generation*, UNHCS, Nairobi; ILO, Geneva.

- United Nations Development Programme (UNDP). 1994. Issues paper for Panel on Urban Poverty and Productive Employment, International Colloquium of Mayors on Social Development, 18-19 August 1994, New York.

- ——. 1997. International Colloquium of Mayors on Governance for Sustainable Growth and Equity, 28-30 July 1997, New York, press release.

- UNEP and The Prince of Wales Business Leaders Forum. 1994. *Partnerships for Sustainable Development: The Role of Business and Industry*, London.

- Vetter, D. 1995. "Financing of human settlements by subnational governments: Opportunities for international cooperation", paper presented at the Conference on Human Settlements in Changing Global Political and Economic Processes, Session on International Cooperation, World Institute for Development Economics Research, United Nations University, Helsinki, 27 August 1995.

- Wood, A. 1994. *North-South Trade, Employment and Inequality*, Clarendon Press, Oxford.

- World Bank. 1979. "National urbanization policies in developing countries, Working Paper No. 347, Washington, D.C.

- ——. 1991. *Urban Policy and Economic Development: An Agenda for the 1990s*, Washington, D.C.

- ——. 1994. *World Development Report: Infrastructure for Development*, Washington, D.C.

- ——. 1995. *World Development Report: Workers in an Integrating World*, Washington, D.C.

- ——. 1997. *World Development Report: The State in a Changing World*, Washington, D.C.

- Zablan, A. 1990. *Vital Issues of the Urban Poor*, Ateneo de Manila, Manila.